THE
SEVEN LAWS
OF MONEY

THE
SEVEN LAWS
OF MONEY

Michael Phillips

with the help of his friends
Salli Rasberry / Jug 'n Candle
Richard Raymond / Stewart Brand

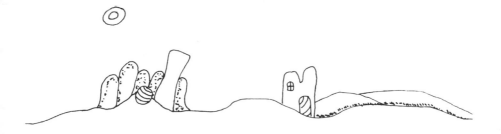

Menlo Park, California / New York.

WORD WHEEL AND RANDOM HOUSE

Drawings by Salli Rasberry

Copyright © 1974   by Michael Phillips

All rights reserved under International and Pan-American Copyright Conventions. Published in the United States by Random House, Inc., New York, and Word Wheel Books, Inc., Menlo Park, California, and simultaneously in Canada by Random House of Canada Limited, Toronto.
Photographs used by permission from the Lick Observatory, University of California, Santa Cruz, California.
"The Last Twelve Hours of the Whole Earth" by Thomas Albright and Charles Perry from Rolling Stone, *Issue # 86, July 8, 1971. Copyright © 1971 by Straight Arrow Publishers, Inc. All Rights Reserved. Reprinted by permission.*

Library of Congress Cataloging in Publication Data

Phillips, Michael, 1938–
The seven laws of money.

1. Money.   2. Finance, Personal.   I. Title.
HG221.3.P5   1974   332'.024   73-20575
ISBN 0-394-49224-3
ISBN 0-394-70686-2 (pbk.)
Manufactured in the United States of America
Typeset by CSC/Pacific, Inc. Palo Alto, California
468975

INTRODUCTION

Many people had been coming to me seeking advice about raising funds for their parent-supported schools. They asked which foundations were the most sympathetic—what were the most likely avenues of support? I always gave the same advice—people energy is far more important than any grant and a good project will always be provided for. Few believed in what I said. My philosophizing didn't pay their rent.

Money seemed such a problem to folks trying to gain control over their own education that I felt a strong commitment to translate my intuitive feeling for money into a form people could deal with. I turned naturally to Michael Phillips who is very knowledgeable about and comfortable with money and gives sound, gentle advice. "Help," I cried "give to us the magic money formula." Michael had been involved with people and their money for over eleven years, and his perspectives are unique. I knew people would trust what he had to say. A former vice-president of a bank and currently business manager of a foundation, he is also president of POINT, the *Whole Earth Catalog* money-giving group which concerns itself more with alliances than the dispersing of coins.

We sat around a tape recorder in Mike's living room with Jug 'n' Candle, Poet and old friend, and out came the basis for *The Seven Laws of Money* . It was typed, copied, and circulated around to everyone from friends in a country community school to executives at the Ford Foundation. The response was overwhelming and The Seven Laws grew into this book.

Michael went to the Library of Congress to make sure there wasn't another Seven Laws of Money book written by another Mike Phillips. What he found was 3,900 books *about* money and not one book which was concerned with the concepts of right livelihood and the forming of alliances; nothing intuitive, sexual or feeling, none incorporating the attitudes we feel are important in our lives and in the lives of the people we admire.

Many friends pulled and tugged, added and took away from this book, helping Michael gather a very warm, personal and well-founded collection of ideas and feelings, offering an entirely new and welcome perspective to the heavily saturated subject of people and their money.

Salli Rasberry
San Francisco 1974

P.S. Michael is a long distance runner.

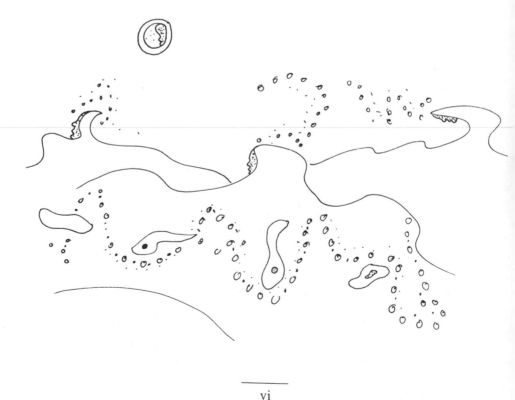

CAST OF CHARACTERS

Stewart Brand

Stewart and I compete, like brothers who are close in age. We play squash and handball. He is well-coordinated, tall and slender. Young Stewart created the *Whole Earth Catalog* at Portola Institute single-handedly. Now he is going to stop war using "war" games. I once said that that's like trying to cure cancer with a Gilbert chemistry set. He said that would probably be how it happens. Stewart is a cybernetician; I think there are only a few dozen in the world. His most visible genius is an innocent, raw honesty. He thinks differently from everyone on nearly everything. Combine this with fearlessness about saying what he feels or what is on his mind, and all of us around him are naked, like the Emperor in his new clothes. Stewart wins the competition for honesty hands down. I'm in there trying.

Salli Rasberry

Salli is one of the most beautiful people I know.

I really know very little biographically about her except that she and Bob Greenway wrote *Rasberry Exercises*. We met two years ago. I got to know her when she was an observer-participant at a National Sex Forum (Glide) ten-day conference. I drove her there daily. We've been in love ever since.

She lives with a few others on a thousand acres near Bodega Bay, north of San Francisco. Until recently she lived in a large teepee on the land, a mythical landscape with extraordinary beauty, fog and rolling hills. She has a horse and an eleven-year-old daughter with the same free spirit as Salli.

Salli is rare. She is a *free* human. Her presence, wisdom, and warmth mean growth to anyone near her.

Dick Raymond

We met shortly after I set up the Market Research and Planning department at the Bank of California in 1966. Dick, a customer of the bank since his days in Portland, had an idea, and after offering it to several people in the bank he was finally routed to me. His idea was that the bank should have luncheons, meetings, etc. for customers so they could meet one another and mutually benefit. I loved the idea. Management took about three years before they tried it; however, even done in the bank's half-assed fashion it worked well. In the meantime, Dick and I started having regular Friday lunches together at a fine Japanese restaurant, to which we each invited a couple of interesting people. The luncheons went on for about three years, during which time Dick started Portola Institute and asked me to join his Board. We have worked closely since.

Dick is physically the image of an "all-American"; he went to Harvard Business School, and gave up a successful business career before I met him. Three more all-Americans like him and no more America! Dick, who is just fifty years old, runs one mile in five minutes and eight miles in fifty minutes comfortably. He has two sets of children, three just out of their teens and with Carol, his wonderful second wife, two pre-schoolers. I find it difficult to describe Dick. He embodies J. Krishnamurti's idea of creative discontent: "As you grow older, keep your discontent alive with the vitality of joy and great affection. Then that flame of discontent will have an extraordinary significance because it will build, create, it will bring new things into being." The father of Portola, the "Briarpatch," and many things to come.

Dick has a conception of karmic differences. This conception resists all attempts of anyone to stuff his morality down someone else's throat. I watch out for that now. Dick has the strongest influence on me.

Jug 'n' Candle

Jug and I met when we were sixteen, sharing a room at the University of Chicago. Jug was an extraordinary mathematician. Once he took a calculus course, read the texts in one night (he had a pattern of staying awake forty-eight hours and sleeping twenty-four), talked for a week about the exquisite "central limit theorem" and took the final exam three months later, getting a perfect score. Jug was a Russian translator for an army spy group, an actuary, and a systems analyst. He comes from Omaha, once had a top secret cryptographic clearance, and became a wandering poet about 1966 after dealing psychedelics at his top secret job in L.A. He is the father of two children, Brother and Sparrow, has a wise short-haired dog, Gitane, travels barefoot around the U. S., riding the rails and living with hobos. Jug usually wears a hat, sleeps in freezing weather outside in his one pair of pants and Navy peajacket. He lives in the briarpatch.

Dick Raymond seems to have coined the phrase "Briarpatch Society." Here's how it's used at Portola Institute:

What is a Briarpatch Society?

In an ultimate sense, the Briarpatch Society consists of people learning to live with joy in the cracks. But, more particularly, if you are positively-oriented and doing (or actively seeking) Right Livelihood, even willing to fail young, and concerned with the sharing of resources and skills with members of an ongoing community (or affinity group), and especially if you see yourself as part of a subsociety that is more committed to "learning how the world works" than to acquiring possessions and status, then you must be a *Briar*.

So howdy, Briar.

CONTENTS

THE
SEVEN LAWS
OF MONEY

THE FIRST LAW

Do it! Money Will Come When
You Are Doing the Right Thing

The First Law is the hardest for most people to accept and is the source of the most distress.

The clearest translation of this in terms of personal advice is "go ahead and do what you want to do." Worry about your ability to do it and your competence to do it but certainly do not worry about the money.

Let me give you a number of examples from my own personal experience where this sort of advice was extremely successful. The Book Fair, The First International San Francisco Book Fair, was being organized, and at the first meeting we became bogged down in the issue of how much to charge and whether the fees we could collect would be enough to cover the cost of the exhibition hall and other expenses. This was a situation where extraordinary people were working together with outstanding ideas and an enormous amount of energy, and they had rapidly become bogged down in the potential agonies of how to plan for money. Fortunately, I was able to say "Don't anybody worry about the money; I'll worry about it." Everybody just looked at me as I said that, and based on my background they accepted it. From that point on money was not discussed by the group except in a very perfunctory way, and as the energies were channeled into the appropriate directions the Book Fair became an outstanding success. At no time either before or during the event was money a problem, as I knew full well would be the case. Since this was

1

an extraordinarily good idea the money just came in. Just rolled in. There was more than enough to pay for everything that was needed.

I have gone to many meetings, listened to many discussions and watched many groups form, start to think about money, start to plan for money, set out to raise the money and then cease to exist. That seems to be the crux of many ventures. They rapidly get bogged down in money and neglect the project and their own personal goals.

I was advising Salli Rasberry on starting a free school. I pointed out that at the first meeting the people involved should deliberately avoid the subject of money, since if they were to discuss how much it would cost to hire teachers, what buildings would cost, etc. their project would likely be doomed at the outset. I suggested that the rules should be interpreted as "do it" and the money would follow. A way to avoid the problem of the first meeting and the general concern about money would be to designate one person or a group of people to worry about money so that other peoples' energies would not become diverted.

Once two men who were planning to start an organization with an interesting idea came to me. They wanted some money to buy a building. I told them that before taking steps to buy a building they needed thirty people or so to sign a piece of paper saying that they were also interested in the organization. By the time the two men came back they had over 250 members in their organization. It had grown to astronomic size in six months. Every once in a while they came back to talk about money. The fact is, with that kind of membership and that kind of energy they have more than adequate resources at their disposal to accomplish anything the group wishes to do, and money is secondary.

The examples I have given have been taken from my role as a consultant in helping groups get started by taking their minds off money. The essential argument, plea, advice here is that if an idea is good enough, and the people involved want it badly enough, they'll begin to put their own personal energy and time into it, and the idea will soon be its own reward. Money itself cannot accomplish their goal; only the people themselves can accomplish it. Maybe that's an abstract interpretation of the law, but it's certainly the result of a great deal of experience. Of the

2

people I have explained this concept to, only a rare few have been able to understand that if they work hard enough on their project money would follow.

Often people say to me "What am I going to do next month? How am I to live until I get this thing started?" What I try to tell them is to get started; go forward; get something done. You have to worry about money for the next month as your own personal problem, in any case. Try to separate the issue of the project you're working on from your own problem of survival. If you're going to predicate the project's survival on your own need to be comfortable for the coming month, you have already doomed the project. Figure out how you're personally going to survive and then, separately, how important the project is to you. You're going to have to continue to support yourself anyway, and when you're working on the project that's an added burden. But the project per se, the success of the project per se, will be seriously jeopardized if you integrate your own need to make a living with the needs of the project.

One of my friends, upon hearing this advice, decided that his particular project was so important to him, and he felt that he could make enough progress on it in two months, that he sold all the books he owned and lived off the revenue for two months. As of now, he has no qualms about that decision. The project was a more than adequate reward.

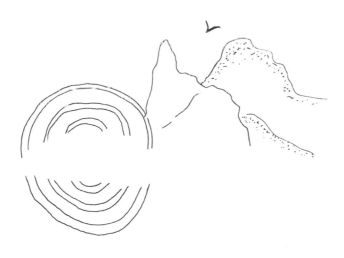

COMMENTARY ON THE FIRST LAW OF MONEY

> Money, which represents the prose of
> life, and which is hardly spoken of in par-
> lors without an apology, is in its effects
> and laws, as beautiful as roses.
>
> Ralph Waldo Emerson, *Nominalist and
> Realist*

Jug once asked me "What is the most difficult thing for people to understand about money?" I thought about it and came to the conclusion that the most difficult thing for people to understand about money is that money will come to you if you are doing the right thing. Money is secondary to what you are doing.

Most of this chapter deals with that statement. I have said it time and again and am always amazed to find that people cannot accept it. Most people can't accept it even when it comes from their own experience. Yet I keep getting more and more evidence to support it and virtually no signs to indicate the opposite.

Many people have argued that what I say is a self-fulfilling prophesy. They say that I can claim that if a project fails or if somebody doesn't get money when they seem to be doing a good job they aren't doing the right thing. Indeed, taken at face value, there is a logical fallacy to this first law. Many people prefer to deal with the logical fallacy of it instead of dealing with its reality.

There are logical fallacies in all the Seven Laws. They cannot be arrived at by a "logical" process. The Seven Laws deal with a part of man that is outside the realm of the typical body of Western thought. You logicians out there will recognize what I mean when I say that it is to be found in Wittgenstein's *Tractus Logicus*; theologians will recognize it by the phrase "transcendental."

The realm of logic in Western man comprises about 2% of his reality. The remaining 98% of reality includes feelings, sex, art, non-verbal communication, most of our sensual inputs, etc. The Seven Laws deal with the operating relationships that exist in the 98% of the world where our logic doesn't apply.

Let me use the example of tariffs to illustrate the divergence between logic as it is used by man and the way the world operates. Ever since the 18th Century, when Adam Smith first began studying economics, it has been very apparent that international tariffs and quotas that exist between countries are not rational or logical. Significantly better arguments can be made for free trade than can ever be made for tariffs. Just briefly, if you are not an economist, the two classical arguments *for* tariffs were "protection of infant industries" and "domestic defense."

An example of what "protection of infant industries" covers is as follows: Let's assume that you want to start a small business. You have discovered that your new business can be carried on profitably. The problem is, though, that the initial cost of *getting into* the business is too great and the prices of your first products would have to be very high. Because they were so high people would continue to buy cheaper products from other countries.

If you rely on logic, the answer to this classic dilemma would not be to impose tariffs but to provide a direct government subsidy to help you start your business.

The argument in favor of "domestic defense" is that we must have our own home oil industries, for example, so that we don't have to rely on other countries in war time. There is a comparable *logical* answer, however, that rules out the need for tariffs.

Throughout history, however, even since Adam Smith and his followers made their rational, clear arguments *for* free trade, we have always had tariffs. During this time there have been enlightened kings, enlightened presidents, and enlightened councils of economic advisors, all fully understanding the logical arguments—yet tariffs have not given way to free trade. To me this is proof that there is something significantly more powerful than logic operating in international economic relations, something that we don't understand. Hopefully, our rationale and our logic will catch up with the facts of reality. All of which leads me back to the First Law of Money and the logical fallacy of it, which is that attempting to understand the law by trying to think about it is not going to be much help. In many ways it is like trying to understand Zen Buddhism through logic rather than feeling. You cannot talk about an experience and expect another person to substitute your words for his lack of experience.

The concept that money "will come to you" is clearly very mystical. Sometimes when one tries to bring something mystical into his daily life the conflict with the world of logic can lead to unusual results.

Several months ago, in offering advice on money, I ran into trouble by using mystical premises. A good friend of mine in the foundation business was planning to leave the country. He had a commitment to a friend of his, a famous lawyer, to raise enough money so that the lawyer could travel and study in Europe for nine months. My friend cajoled me into accepting responsibility for raising the $8,000 needed. The reason he wanted someone to take this responsibility was to enable the lawyer to continue to work on an important law suit and not be diverted by worrying about money.

I met the lawyer and made it clear to him that I would accept the responsibility; first, however, I had a nominal number of things for him to do. The actual words I used were "I will accept the responsibility for seeing that you get the money. I don't guarantee with absolute certainty that you'll get the amount you want, but you should go ahead and do exactly what you're supposed to do and plan the trip on the assumption that you will have the money." That was it. On two occasions, after I had done some investigation, I asked him to write letters. At one point I wrote him a letter suggesting he do two specific things.

About six weeks before his trip was to begin he phoned in the evening and insulted me in the most incredible terms I had heard in years. The gist of his fury was that although I had said I would help him raise the money, I had done nothing at all, while he had spent an enormous amount of time and had worried endlessly trying to raise the money. After he had calmed down a little, I found out that he had not done most of the things I had asked him to do because he had doubted my ability to raise money. It turned out that he was willing to call and berate me because he had *gotten* a grant. As the reader may have guessed, the grant had come from one of the first people I had told him to send a letter to.

I was sorry about the whole matter. The lawyer operated in a very logical and goal-oriented world, highly planned in monetary terms, expecting me to do a lot of running around, while I had operated on my mystical premise in accepting this particular responsibility.

This is an example both of how the First Law works and of how recommending that someone else operate on the basis of the First Law can lose you a few friends. People who have strong, money-oriented goals are not going to accept this almost mystical view. If you are as foolish as I was, and try to be an intermediary between their goals and some other responsibility you may lose a friend too.

During my discussion of the First Law with Salli Rasberry, Salli asked about getting a project started. My response emphasized the importance of separating the project from survival problems. The two need not be separated, however, if survival is integrated with the project in a unique way. The concept behind this is the concept of "right livelihood."

You may be reading this book from the perspective of a person trying to carry out a project to build a windmill or a diving bell, or trying to figure out how to get to the Middle East so you can walk to Mecca on your knees. On the other hand, you may be reading simply because you want to know "How do I get a job? How do I save up enough money to buy a car, pay the bills, and get enough money to buy some milk for the baby?" There is, in my mind, a distinction between these, and the separation occurs when the project is different from and independent of you, when it is distinct in your own mind from what you consider to be a "living." To take the example of the diving bell: if the diving bell is for pleasure or for looking at fish, it is part of a project; on the other hand, if you are an ichthyologist who makes his living photographing fish and writing about them, then the diving bell is part of your livelihood. My advice is that you should recognize that you are always going to have to eat, that you are going to have to survive the next week, month, or hour, and that you should distinguish the priority of the project from your day-to-day work. Unfortunately, many people can't separate the two, and the net result is that their belief that the project they are working on is the most important thing they can do gets coupled with their conviction that they have to survive. The combination of these two ideas leads them to believe that *the world owes them a living.*

I question whether mankind has reached the stage where we can view everyone as deserving financial support for his lifetime. Our current view is that children, the mentally retarded and senile, as well as the physically ill and disabled, are entitled to support. Whether in time that will expand to include more people, I don't know. At the present time, in your own particular case, I think it is best to consider whether you are capable both of providing for yourself and doing your project too.

The matter is quite different when your livelihood and your desired activities are integrated; this is where the concept of right livelihood enters. Right livelihood is something I learned from Dick Baker, a Zen Buddhist Roshi. I don't know its origins, and I'm not certain of its history. I can't tell you directly whether you are involved in right livelihood. However, I can suggest some of the questions you might ask yourself. Please don't take me too literally—this is not a typical Cosmopolitan questionnaire to measure something like whether you are gay or straight sexually. It is simply a way to give you a perspective on what right livelihood is.

First of all, do you think you can undertake your work for a long time? Right livelihood could be spending a whole life as a carpenter, for example. One of the qualities of right livelihood is that within it, within the practice of it, is the perfection of skills and qualities that will give you a view of the universe. Constant perfection or practice of a right livelihood will give you a view of the whole world, in a sense similar to Hemingway's story of *The Old Man and the Sea.* In Hemingway's story the old man's life as a fisherman gives him a connection with the entire world, and a "whole world of experience." What are the rewards? Right livelihood has within itself its own rewards; it deepens the person who practices it. When he is twenty years old he is a little different from the person he will be at thirty, and he will be even more different when he's forty, and fifty. Aging works *for* you in right livelihood. It's like a good pipe or a fine violin; the more you use it the deeper its finish.

Another thing you can ask yourself about right livelihood is whether the good intrinsic in your livelihood is also good in terms of the greater community. This is a hard question to answer when you are asking it about yourself. It's hard to establish criteria, but a carpenter can certainly be doing good for the community in a very powerful sense. All of this is by way of saying that you shouldn't separate the idea of doing good from whatever your livelihood is; they can be integrated. With a right livelihood you would not be doing what you are doing and at the same time be saying "I'd rather be a nurse, I would rather be head of the Red Cross." The dichotomy would not be necessary. What you would be doing, in your eyes, would be as beneficial to the community as any other function.

I have tried to give a few guidelines on right livelihood. However, experience is a part of livelihood that cannot be described in words. The words and phrases I use are necessarily trivial descriptions, such as your job and you are "centered," or the relationship between who you are and what you do is "focused." These are clichés, and they miss the point. But they give you a hint in the same sense that stained glass windows give you a hint of a rainbow.

Right livelihood is a concept that places money secondary to what you are doing. It's something like a steam engine, where the engine, fire and water working together create steam for forward motion. Money is like steam; it comes from the interaction of fire (passion) and water (persistence) brought together in the right circumstance, the engine.

The concept of money as something of secondary importance if you are doing the right thing has not been difficult for me to accept. A good example comes from my personal life.

In my late teens I tried to decide whether to be an artist or to follow another career. I asked one of my mother's friends, a very respected and well-known sculptor, to look at my paintings and tell me whether I could be an artist. What he said when he looked at them was: "They are very nice. Whether you are an artist or not is not visible. It depends on whether you can work eight hours a day every day." It happens that he was a Japanese sculptor, maybe with a touch of Zen training.

I know that if I were to work eight hours a day at my art, within four or five years I would be able to make a living at it. With that much time, energy, devotion and self-focusing, what I am would emerge in my art sufficiently to be recognized as having value. I don't see that as different from a man who goes into the business world or who works in his grocery store eight hours a day. He certainly has to expect to work at what he is doing, to develop his skills and to make a living at it, and he can't expect it to take much less than five years.

If you are devoted enough and can find enough passion within yourself, you will find an almost infinite number of ways to make a living at the things you want to do. The way this book is being done is an example; it embodies my advice to artists—the hardest group for me to deal with in explaining the First Law.

Publishing this book is an example of how artists can form a structure to ensure their right livelihood. *The Seven Laws of Money* is being co-published by Word Wheel, a group of artists and writers. My agreement is that half of the profits will go to Word Wheel (and the rest Random House). Thirty percent of the royalties will go to POINT and the rest to me, Jug and a few others. Word Wheel is an example of artists getting together, believing in each other and having enough trust to publish as a cooperative; they realize they work more efficiently that way and that each one will benefit from the combination of all their skills and experience.

POINT, whose origins are in the surplus money from the *Whole Earth Catalog* created by Stewart Brand, is a non-profit foundation that gives grants. Stewart is an extraordinary artist who felt he owed a little bit to the community. Since he had received the $20,000 it cost him to start the *Catalog* as a gift, he decided to give $20,000 in cash in $100 bills back to the community. (See description of the Demise Party at the end of the Fifth Law). The rest of the money Stewart put into a non-profit foundation to be used for community good. It is clear to me that Stewart understood that his success was not a result of preordained, divine selection in the classic Calvinist sense, but that among artists there is fate, or a chance likelihood that one, or two, or three out of ten are going to be selected by the public, or the people with money, to be successful.

If an artist recognizes that reaching financial success is mostly a matter of fate rather than a matter of talent, and he can find other people who agree with him, he has tremendous leverage. What can be done then is powerful. A group of relatively unknown artists who consider themselves peers can form a small non-profit institution. Within five years it is almost a certainty that, if they indeed form a pool of talent better than the average, money will flow in. Maybe the group has the talents of the Rod McKuen, Jonathan Living ston Seagull type; maybe their talents are more similar to Hemingway's or T. S. Eliot's. In either case, within five years that group is going to see revenue coming in, and probably they can all live on it.

Aside from furnishing a source of income, there are two advantages to this kind of group. The first is a recognition that selection by the economic forces of the market place is not necessarily a recognition of innate talent. The second is that the reward of money from the market place should not be taken as a key as to how the artist should develop his skills. There have been many fine artists who were rewarded monetarily when they were still relatively young and who subsequently did not develop much beyond that point (Dali, Stravinsky, Hans Hoffman). They continued to produce what they were most rewarded for, and their art, or their talent, became stereotyped and did not progress. In many ways this can be avoided by a cooperative group effort because the individual can continue to produce what he is best capable of. If he is on his own and he gets rewarded by ten, fifty or a hundred thousand dollars from the sale of a work of art, it is almost inevitable that his next work of art is going to be very similar, and so on and so on as the rewards come in.

One of the most extraordinary events involving right livelihood that I have ever known was the effect of Stewart Brand's decision not to continue publishing the *Whole Earth Catalog*. He stopped for a number of reasons, all of which were explained in the *Catalog*—the primary one being that he felt he had published it long enough. The decision to cut off publication with the *Last Whole Earth Catalog* turned out to be one of the great marketing inventions of all time; the catalog, which might have sold over ten years at the rate of 100,000 to 200,000 copies a year, has sold over 1,100,000 copies in two years. Stewart is considerably happier than he would have been if he were still producing the catalog or watching some staff do a half-rate imitation of what he started.

There's an interesting connection I'd like to point out between doing "the right thing" and getting a bank loan. Banks are highly mysterious organizations to just about everybody, including bankers. (The mystery helps to cover up the difference between the good bankers and the bad ones.) I have a number of private business clients right now, and I often take them to the bank to get loans. One of the things that I have found about a good banker is that he does not make purely rational judgments. He does expect each client to have loan papers and related material in good order—not because the papers or the numbers on them have particular magical significance but because the client's ability to perceive the importance of these papers are all reflections on himself. A good bank loan officer will always say that he makes his loan decision on the "quality" of the borrower. A "quality" borrower is one who is wholly integrated into the function for which he is seeking a loan and is perfectly capable of what he has set out to do. I make sure myself that my client has these qualities before I send him into a bank. (Banks are cold and austere, and many of the loan officers I've known have been grumpy, nasty, insensitive people. Only a few of them are able to understand, sympathize and intuitively evaluate the potential borrower as a person.) A client will be judged on whether or not the business is meeting the needs of its community—because if it is it will be rewarded with profits.

I fear that I may have misled a few readers with some of my examples. I can see where some one might say, "Well, I'll drop some acid, snort a lot of coke and get on with my thing and not worry about money." I can also hear some other readers saying, "First I've got to sit and meditate on what the right thing is, and second get things going smoothly around here so that everything is running perfectly. Then third, I want this house spotless, and fourth, I want everybody to be spiffy and well-dressed. Then the money will just come driving up the turnpike when everything is looking cool and clean."

Now maybe these two approaches will work, but what I am driving at is a little different. My authority does not come from a rational point of view, and I could be wrong, so I certainly hope nobody reading this book takes it as gospel. My understanding of the First Law of Money is that a person's focus must be on his passion. He must be able to integrate who he is with what he is doing, see his project as a whole, and do his work systematically in order to legitimately expect the money to take on its secondary "helping" role.

The analogy that comes to mind when I think of this middle ground between avoiding money and focusing on it is the eye. In order for you to see, your eye cannot be perfectly still. The eye itself vibrates. If it stops or is held it overloads, and there is no image either. For the image to appear you need some combination of stability and movement. The same applies to money.

Jug 'n' Candle provides an interesting example of this. He lives on very little and virtually never works for money, knowing that if he doesn't get a meal within the next two or three hours he can go a day or two or three without food. This attitude gives him enormous flexibility. Instead of having to think of the streets of Venice as the only place to find a meal, his kind of perspective gives him the whole range of Southern California as a source of food. If he felt he had to eat at 6:00 p.m. sharp he might not get food very often. He would probably get so wrapped up in the meal-getting process, would get so hassled by it, that people wouldn't love him as a poet nor be as likely to give him a meal in the first place just for the fun of having him around.

There is something else I want to discuss under the First Law—the life cycle and money. It is helpful to remember that once we were all children, unable to support ourselves, and that at some point again before our deaths most of us will be physically unable to provide a living for ourselves. In between these periods, the issue of providing sustenance for ourselves and others becomes an issue. It is interesting that in most cultures there are periods of apprenticeship and low wages, and there is a period of increasing wages prior to retirement. In the United States, if one looks at a simple chart of income distribution it is very skewed; it looks unfair because the 20% of the population which has the highest wages earns 80% of the income. However, when one looks at the distribution in terms of life cycle, comparing people in their twenties to those in their fifties and correcting for the fact that over their worklife the income of the younger ones significantly increases, then the unfairness (inequality of income) seems almost to disappear.

In your own life there should be some recognition that you are probably going to live quite a while. You can change your horizons when you realize this. You will have fewer immediate desires and probably a greater potential to find out what you want to do. As you get older your ability to survive and your rapport with other people will undoubtedly be a reflection of your comfort with yourself and your awareness of who you are. All of which suggests that it makes sense to think in a fairly broad perspective and to realize that when you are young it is very unlikely that you are going

---

to have a substantial amount of money unless you inherit it, and that then is the time to accept your status, develop your skills, potentials and qualities. It's summed up in a phrase that Portola Institute developed: "A willingness to fail young."

Salli Rasberry, who worked on this book with me, asked me to elaborate on people who come to me with the knowledge that I am going to advise them to go ahead and do what they do best, and the money will come. There seem to be three different reasons why they ask for my advice:

1) There are some who want to hear it from me personally so they can accept it for reasons of authority.
2) Some think that accepting it will lead to direct results, that maybe because I am a foundation man I will be so impressed with their hard work that I will give them a grant.
3) Finally, there are some who don't really know it but *think* they do—and want endorsement.

In the latter case I am reminded of a story about a psychologist who used a test on business executives to determine how successful they might turn out to be. One of the pictures he used in the test depicted a man on a rope, which he would ask the executives to describe. If the executive described the man as climbing the rope, he was judged to be aggressive and successful. If the man on the rope was described as simply hanging on, the executive was judged to be a man who was interested primarily in trying to maintain his job and who thus wouldn't get very far in the company. If the executive described the man on the rope as climbing down, he had really made up his mind to quit the company, or to retire.

An article about the test and the picture of the man on the rope was published in *Time*. Shortly thereafter, one of the psychologist's patients came in and said he had read the *Time* article and that he knew what the answer should be. "Well, that man is going up," he said. "I know he's supposed to be going up. He's probably going up because there's a lion at the bottom of the rope snapping at his feet."

Clearly, he knew the direction the man should go, but he didn't understand the ideas behind the interpretation of the picture.

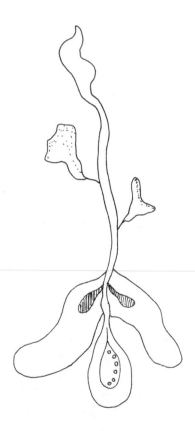

Nakamura Letter

The following letter deals directly with right livelihood. The writer is H. Nakamura, who in his early years was to marry a member of the Japanese royal family but who chose instead to become a carpenter. This letter was written to Dick Baker, a Roshi of the San Francisco Zen Center. Mr. Nakamura wished to come to the United States to teach.

Tokyo
May 10, 1973

My dear sir Baker,

My broken English is about 50 years old, since I graduated the middle school. So it is Japenglish, I say.

My elder sister said her letter always, she is living very happily at Zen Center, every day. I have paid respect to your personality, from bottom of my heart, and thank you warmly for your kindness.

Now, I want to go to your country, availing myself of your kindness. I have many hope, idea, and planning to the visiting to your country.

One of them, it is teaching about technique of furniture and interior decoration (Japanese style or international style), and how to master of their design.

But, student must be intent on their studies about Art. It mean and include artistic spirit, artistic conscience, art impulse, and art instinct . . . Art is not best, but if man can not appreciate to Art, it is like non smell wine, no colored sky or river. The student needs to study or Art, in course of catch strictly and deep personality.

At first, these mind of man is the fatal enemy to himself, that is tricks, wiles, artfulness, knowing, smarts . . . Student must learn and study about picture, sculpture, music, literature, arts and crafts, man and woman.

In this way, student will reach easily more higher or deeper of his spirit, like the diamond in the sky. If anyone who do not like to study thus art field, he shall be resigned to his fate, he is only a worker of tricks, wiles, artfulness.

On the way study Art, student must touch the core with his firm believe. Case by case, A and B and C, he must decide it immediately good or not of arts essence and real, when he met or saw it only a glance like thunder. To Art, this manner he must continue it always in his life, until his death. Thus his personality grow a grass, a tree . . . or pyramid.

First of all, most important aim, it is his mental attitude to Nature study. He must concerned with mountain, rivers, trees, birds, animals, fishes, insect, sky and ocean . . . and man. Is man soul of all creation? It is not true exactly. Man is a point on the earth, he is an equal footing like a pointer. And one of the most alarming animal in this world, it is man. This is regrettable truth. So I think and wish that, we must listen and admiring or look on with admiration, to the system of nature, with gentle manner.

On these learning and study, he can reach nearly perfect mind, spirit, and mentality. Where there is a will, there is a way.

Many words of this letter, it is only my practical experience and endeavor. This is a little seed of mine, I do not like lean against text book. One must sow before one can reap.

Advice to Friends

I am often asked to give advice to friends on the management of their personal funds. The advice I give is a conceptual twist on the First Law. The friend should invest in what he personally knows best. Two examples:

1) Ruth, in her forties, inherited some money, which, added to her and her husband's savings, gave them $20,000 to invest. She took my advice and put most of the money in two things she knows well—publishing and her daughter. The publishing venture will soon break even and most likely will do well. Most importantly, she loves it. Her daughter opened a small retail outlet selling mountaineering equipment and started a wholesale import business. She did fairly well, had a lot of fun and gained a great deal of experience. Ironically, Ruth's husband's dry cleaning business expanded as a direct result of his daughter's store.

2) My father, a former rabbi, became a teacher of anthropology in his late forties. Although he wasn't very good at business he was planning to invest in apartment buildings to give him income when he retired. I talked him out of it, and the net result was that upon retirement he sold his house and is now using his savings to travel around the world and teach in countries where people over 65 can still teach. Of course he's having a wonderful time.

There are countless other examples. I would always recommend that a person who knows wine should put his money in wine or vineyards rather than Standard Oil stock. Of course people have trouble accepting the value of their own experience. It is hard for a man who has valued wine most of his life to realize that wine is a good area to invest in—because he knows all the problems of that field. There is no limit to which I could carry this logic. Regardless of what field an individual has expertise in—appaloosa horses, native wild flowers, florentine marble, or Wobbly folk songs —that's where he should invest if he has money to invest. The hardest part is using imagination to find investments that relate directly to his expertise.

Dick

The following is a list of organizational fallacies compiled by Dick Raymond upon the occasion of the formation of POINT Foundation. Don't take it too straight. Dick wrote it for his friends, and it embodies a lot of humor for us when we think of the many smooth-talking people he has in mind for such statements as "saying something well is the equivalent to doing something well."

1) *Create a role model and it will be adopted by others throughout the land.* No, it won't—at least not voluntarily. There may be, in fact, a greater propensity in the human animal to reject or resist "successful models" than to adopt them, except possibly under conditions of coercion. Role models may stimulate groups to do something of their own which they have wanted to do—but in their own way

2) *If you launch a well-designed project it will cause people to change their beliefs or habits and become participants and supporters.* No. Crusaders' missions simply don't evoke converts as we think. The process of bending the minds of others is much more intricate than any of us comprehends, in my opinion.

3) *Do experimentation, and when the bugs are worked out you can establish a program that will operate on a continuing basis.* No, that's like Christianity; the fallacy is in thinking that the experiment is finished, when in actuality it never stops. A precaution is very much in order: beware of permanence, which is usually a synonym for rigidity or decadence.

4) *There are many original ideas and unique activities that merit support.* Not so. Surprisingly few people carry any kind of fantasy around with them; still fewer have fantasies that can generate support.

5) *Ideas that can be persuasively articulated by a well-informed spokesman can be competently administered by that spokesman or by someone hired as an administrator.* Watch out. Competent administrators are nearly as rare as saints, especially in the field of non-profit work. (Incompetence is most severely felt in the important function of financial control.)

6) *The best way to stretch foundation dollars and to broaden the support for proposed projects is to insist on matching funds.* Bullshit. The matching funds rarely appear, and the project goes limping into the world with half a chassis and no engine.

7) *With nice buildings and equipment you tend to symbolize and identify the project.* Very deceptive reasoning. You will probably identify with an audience you don't really want (you attract identity-seekers rather than contributing participants). Also, you are soon possessed by the property and not vice versa.

8) *Encourage staff participation in decision-making and planning and they will then understand the operation as a whole and will act wisely in fulfilling their role within the broader scope.* This is a classic half-truth, and unfortunately I'm still groping for the missing half. Probably the idea of participative decision-making is an attractive slogan in search of a solid theory to support it.

---

9) *Saying something well is the equivalent of doing something well.* By now we all recognize this immortal fallacy (don't we?) It is so loaded with deception that it is almost elegantly evil. It hides hypocrisy, karmic difference, and man's instinct for crap-detection, but still continues to go on unchallenged from one generation to the next.

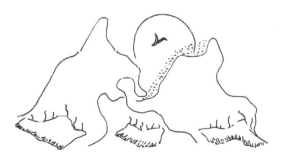

Jug

Ask YOURSELF

Is
Money
Real?

In the olden times money was

wampum
beads
something pretty
found or beautified

And even today sometimes you get your
shit together
righteously
by searching
through alleys and the local dump or
if you're on the land you find

pinecones
or maybe herbs
and roots
good to eat
strong
medicine

you do your thing upon what you have
found and trade
it
is

Creation of Money

a case of the

Energy into Beauty

transformation

Or could be you wake up in the morning

nothing on your mind
                                 and settle upon
breakfast as a reason to be so you maybe
seek out someone or someplace you know
has baked some bread and say

                My that smells good!

or whatever is on your lips

childlike
                 sing
                      and receive bread

(because bread seeks to be eaten)

"What would I do with a pile of bread?
Ten, twenty thousand dollars, money like
that? I'd buy a Porsche, because I like to drive
— driving six or seven hours a day is a joy to me."

                    —truck driver

So maybe you jess keep on trucking

balling the jack
                    and in that case
you
            KNOW
               you are always going to eat

"If you've got too much money buy a car.
I've never known anyone who has a car with
any money."

                    —hitchhiker

If you are among those who say

It ain't easy!

we have evolved for you
according to certain misty principles

The

Seven

Laws

of

Money

These are not laws like

Do Not Go Broke
or
Debters go to Jail

These are laws in accord with

Forgive us our debts
and
We Forgive our debters

These are laws like

Water falls on
friends
     and at the same time strangers

Did someone ask

      Of what use are such laws
      in a world like this?

"Look at that, a flashing neon wonder,
it says 69, 69, is that the time?"

"Bullshit, it's forty something. I'm
freezing my ass. Wish we'd get a ride."

The world is ever changing but the

      Seven Laws of Money

change very slowly and will still work

for you or against you
                 when the
numbers
flashing on the Stock Brokers' window

flash no more
           (the day may come)
or EVEN when the Exchange hits
         Two Thousand and Two

behind that an omnilateral total and
complete disarmament treaty has just been
signed by all heads of state and also,
we hope, by you.

"Look at that. It says UP. It's going
up, whatever it is."

THE
SECOND LAW

MONEY HAS ITS OWN RULES:
Records, Budgets, Saving, Borrowing

The rules of money are probably Ben Franklin-type rules, such as never squander it, don't be a spendthrift, be very careful, you have to account for what you're doing, you must keep track of it, and you can never ignore what happens to money.

The high priests of money, particularly of Law Two, are obviously accountants. Maybe we should have a cult in which accountants are worshipped; projects related to that cult would probably be very successful. Maybe we don't think about the magic and spectacular mysticism implicit in what accountants do. Accountants can handle the books of General Motors in exactly the same way that they can do the most bizarre free school, and from their point of view there is little difference. One may be a little more complex than the other but they are done exactly the same way.

What does an accountant do? He looks at what is coming in, he records the sources of income, he sees what records are kept and examines all the details of how monies were expended. He studies the records to see how the money flowed through and where it was stored at any particular time. He uses such things as an income and expense statement or an asset and liability statement. These are simply records of the flow of money kept in accurate detail by general categories. The rule of money is that you just can't hand several people checks and say go ahead, write the checks you want on this checking account; you can't! Someone has to be responsible for knowing what check was written, where it went and where the funds were coming from. Those are the rules of money and they are absolute.

How does this translate into the daily life of operating projects? First, all expenses must be kept track of, *all* expenses, and where a receipt is possible a receipt should be kept. It's possible for you to set some lower limit below which it's not necessary to keep extremely detailed accounts; if you're really poor that might mean keeping careful track of everything over fifty cents. If you're rich you might keep careful track of everything over ten dollars. Once you set this minimum for record keeping you must observe it. If, at any time, you should get lost in your record keeping, say after two months, and you find you're stuck and things don't balance, you have to stop what you're doing, go back, and straighten it out step by step until it is correct.

Most inexperienced people make the mistake of ignoring this essential rule of money, and many sophisticated people do too. I have one client in particular who has a very successful firm. Last year the client was in very serious trouble and invited me in as a consultant. The first thing I did was to have an accountant prepare a careful analysis of the firm's expenses and a month to month record over a six month period of what the company had been doing. I also had a careful set of books drawn up for the company. What this client had been doing without being the slightest bit conscious of it was to go deeper and deeper in the hole every month. He wasn't even aware of it. The cash flow was fine, he always seemed to have just enough cash in the bank, he always seemed to be just meeting his payroll and he didn't worry about it. His sales continued to grow. The fact is that when I came in he was in debt on his books by more than $15,000 and getting deeper in debt. Less than a year later that debt had been totally wiped out and the principals were at least $15,000 richer in a visible monetary way. This is not preposterous or an extreme example. It is quite common for businesses to be insensitive to money problems and the requirements of money, assuming that just because it's coming in they are profitable and doing well.

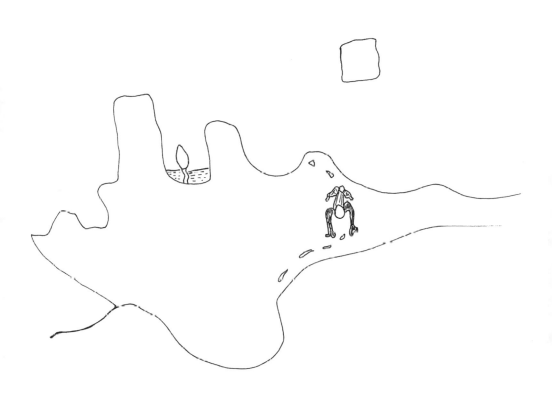

Money Rules

So first we empty our pockets
count
(an act of imagination)
Draw a Line

Here we have   and over here we have

31¢   6¢

we need for a short dog

"Brother, could your spare six cents?
We are trying to get us a bottle."

Accountants call it "Accrual"
(don't ask why)
there's two ways to go

Cash basis   or   Accrual

Accrual is how the big corporations and other
governments do. When they send out their billing
they put it down in Black Ink   UP
thinking

That's how it's done.

The Russians do the same and call it a "Plan".
Cash basis is
thinking
DOWN
sending
a bill to someone you don't think will pay.
Cash basis to the accountant is a fiction.

So is accrual. Take your pick.

———

We can't list the rules of money, unfortunately, because they are more like an ethic than a list. They do not tell you what to do, like an abacus where you add when two beads are down and subtract when three beads are up. The rules tell you that in certain situations, by following a particular line of behavior, there will be certain beneficial consequences, and things will turn out okay in the long run. Like all ethics, the rules operate at many levels. If you fail at one level, they tell you what level to go to next. It's a comprehensive system, a macramé hanging that weaves in and out of your mind. We can all see some of the main strands, and the knots that are impossible to untangle.

The first and clearest rule is that you have to keep track of your money. You have to know approximately how much you have, how much you are spending, how much is coming in, and what the general direction of your dollar flow is. A good diversion at this point, necessary to help keep track of money, is to have an idea of what in mathematics is called "significant digits." If you didn't learn it in high school, it can be summarized in a few words: any form of measurement has some degree of precision beyond which increased precision is of no use and below which lack of precision makes the entire venture useless.

Let me give you a personal example. My oldest daughter, Cynthia, says it's "about a mile" from my house to my ex-wife Helen's house, where she lives. What she's saying is that it takes approximately five minutes by car, ten to twelve minutes walking. For her, a mile is essentially a rounded-off measure; she talks in terms of half a mile, a mile, one and a half miles, and so on. She's rounding off the distance by approximately half a mile. That is useful in terms of the amount of time and the type of traveling she and I do, since the only two means of travel we use between the two houses are foot and car. If Cynthia were flying over that same distance, however, the distance between the two houses would be so insignificant it would hardly be mentionable. The houses would appear to be right next to each other. If she were pushing a wheelbarrow of heavy stuff, or moving a refrigerator from one house to the other on a dolly, the fact that it is actually 4,800 feet instead of "a mile" would be of some consolation, in the same sense that the front stairway having 20 steps instead of 26 would be of some consolation. On the other hand, if I were laying a wire between the two houses for an intercom it would be very significant for me to know the number of feet within at least fifty feet. (It would be useless for me to know it within a few inches, because there would be at least that much stretch in the wire.) I hope that gives you an idea of what "significant digits" are. They are a measure of precision relative to what you are doing.

In terms of the use of money there is something comparable to "significant digits" when you keep track of expenditures. If you earned $30,000 a year, for example, and had savings of $10,000 it probably wouldn't make any difference if you didn't keep track of the total of one day's expenses when you were shopping in Acapulco. Forgetting about a couple of hundred dollars wouldn't be too serious. If you had planned in advance that the total week-long trip would cost you, say $1,700, being off by two hundred dollars would just mean taking a little more out of your savings account. However the opposite would be the case if your income were only $7,000 and your savings were small. A misjudgement of two hundred dollars could take you as much as six months to replace in your savings, six months in terms of cutting costs and taking peanut butter and jelly sandwiches for lunch.

There are certain types of work involving precision that deal more with the ethic of money and less with the significant digit aspects. I have to confess that when I was a banker I allowed myself one form of petty larceny: when I went to a business lunch I would include a 35 cent Garcia y Vega cigar on my luncheon tab. Sometimes I even allowed myself two or three, depending upon how many I thought I would smoke that day. The total bill, of course, was picked up by my bank expense account. I could certainly come up with ten or fifteen rationalizations as to why that was perfectly okay, but that's irrelevent. Within the money ethic it is not okay for the banker to perpetrate any form of larceny, even if it amounts to only 35 cents.

In England, what I did is called a "fiddle." British folklore says that every man has his fiddle; it's the tiny bit of cheating he does.

The important point I want to bring out here is that the cheating should be within some controllable emotional limit. When I became treasurer of the Glide Foundation, knowing that I readily had access to several million dollars (to potentially be able to abscond with it), I stopped the cigar bit and made sure that all expense bills were accurate to within 5 cents. When I go out to lunch now I am very careful to make a note of the precise amount, and if I don't remember for sure I underestimate it. There's some danger point that triggers in everybody's mind a feeling of "Well, I've done a little bit; maybe I'll do a little bit more the next time," and you have to know what that trigger point is. With me, when there are several million dollars I could potentially steal, five cents is that trigger point. When I was a banker and could steal very little but *could* abuse an expense account to the tune of two or three thousand dollars a year, 35 cents was the trigger point I allowed myself.

An example of a man who didn't know his trigger point is Fred, an embezzler who was working in the operations department of our bank. When he was finally caught everyone was completely surprised. Fred was a very meek man in his late fifties, shy, quiet, retiring. He was very pleasant. Fred was always given a relatively secure job. We all relied on him to do his work, knowing he wouldn't create trouble and that he'd be around for a long time.

In the early 1950's, when he was a low-level employee, probably a head teller, Fred had begun to make some money on his own in uranium stock, the kind that was being sold out of Salt Lake City. He was so happy and proud of himself that he began telling his friends to buy uranium stock. As the stock rose in value he encouraged more and more of his friends to buy more and more stock. His friends began to see him as some sort of financial genius, and many of them sold their personal belongings, borrowing along with him to invest in uranium stock. However, the uranium bubble soon burst, and nearly everybody involved lost significant amounts of money. Most of Fred's friends set about learning to live with their losses, but Fred felt that their losses were some sort of reflection on him as a person. He became generous with his friends, taking them to lunch, giving them gifts —initially within his salary, within his ability to pay. Before long, though, he began to feel that his gifts were a poor substitute for the losses his friends had suffered. Fred began to embezzle on a small scale—a little bit of cash here, a little bit of cash there.

As his job responsibilities within the bank increased, he progressed to a position where he was in charge of the bank control accounts, one of the core parts of banking. This is the "account" which adjusts the total amount of money that a bank handles every day so that balance sheets come out equal on both sides. Not only was he in charge of this account; he also learned how to embezzle from it.

Over an eight to ten year period he came to realize that nobody could check his system, since he was the only one who fully understood it. Whenever anybody came in to examine the books he was always there. He almost never took a vacation, because he didn't dare teach anybody how to handle the bank control account. He was taking increasingly more money, gambling occasionally to try to win to pay it back but usually using it to buy back worthless uranium stock from his friends.

Fred was caught because he finally went on vacation, and while he was gone someone *had* to figure out his books. It was discovered that he had taken $300,000.

This is what I consider a fairly typical case. I mention it because it deals with the trigger point of emotional control. There is some point for everyone at which they can no longer control themselves.

While we're on the subject of embezzlement I'd like to mention something my mother, who is a radical, used to say: "People who steal bread to feed their familes are the ones who go to jail, and people who steal hundreds of millions (in the form of profits) are the ones who succeed." Wonderful as she is, I disagree with her on this. Certainly a high percentage of poor people who steal bread *do* get caught and *do* get punished. However, it doesn't follow that actually stealing *money* on a large scale is unpunishable. The folk phrase she is quoting confuses Marxist views of profit with actual theft. This view is based on the assumption that if someone *else* has more money than you there must be something wrong. He must have gotten it by doing something bad (like stealing). Or, more abstractly, what he did to get it (earn profits) is bad.

In fact, the more money you steal, the more likely you are to get caught. Large-scale theft is in some ways a less rational crime to commit than murder. Why? Because if you kill somebody, the pain of the people affected (the relatives and friends) dies out in time. Five years after someone's friend is murdered the anguish is gone, but five years after somebody has stolen $700,000 there remains a reason for finding that person and getting that money back. Crimes of violence lead to a resolution of emotions. Crimes involving money don't lead to anything but perpetual desire to get the money back. It might appear that it would be easy to hide the theft of $700,000 by fleeing to Brazil, but all of the benefits of stealing it in the first place would have evaporated. The thief would be in perpetual hiding, since the people who lost the money would probably be willing to spend up to half the amount to recover it. A hundred thousand dollars is enough to find almost anybody anywhere in the world, or at least to make life so miserable that the thief would never enjoy the fruits of his stealing.

An interesting aspect of pursuing embezzlers is the attitude of insurance companies and other companies involved with fraud. Something not publicized, but known to most criminologists and people involved in prosecuting thieves, is that if it's clear and demonstrated but not provable that a particular person stole money, it is considered appropriate to "frame" him and put him in jail for a term as long as he would have served for the actual crime. For example, if you stole a large sum from the bank and the investigator knew for certain that you had stolen it but couldn't prove it, you can be certain you'd be kidnapped and would turn up in some Mediterranean country with dope on you, some place where dope is punishable by ten years in jail.

They feel it would be would be worth it to pay several thousand dollars to fly you there and leave you in that condition. There is a presumption within the fraud field that every thief must be punished. The principle for this is that the people who are tracking you down must be dissuaded from the temptation of stealing themselves, since they are often in the position to do so.

This started with a discussion of the trigger point that each person needs to find out about in order to keep him from the temptation that leads to financial crime. I covered a range of topics designed to scare you—to let you know that smart people don't embezzle and that the forces working against the embezzler are powerful. (I think I overdid it.)

Back to the ethics of money, its rules, and paying attention to it.

Part of "paying attention" to your money deals with debt. By debt I mean both large loans and small bills, the latter being situations where you have used something (gas, phone, space, etc.) and owe the institution that sold it to you. Having debts and paying bills is not only useful but in many instances an effective way of making you "pay attention" to money, helping you to control yourself. Let me explain that in more detail.

When I was a banker I did a study on the potential market for an automatic bill-paying service for the bank's customers. I found out that people have a very strong resistance to automatic bill paying. Ostensibly, their reason was that they didn't want the bank to get involved in their personal life. Knowing how much anguish is involved in bill paying, however, I doubted that was the real reason. Probing further into how people pay their bills, I found that bill paying had several interesting hidden qualities. First of all, people used their bill paying as a way of punishing other people. A dentist or an interior decorator who hadn't done a very good job was certain not to receive payment for two, three or six months. This use of money as a form of punishment in the payment of bills was something people actually relished.

The second interesting thing was that people like to know the total amount of their bills, because this acts as a brake, a way of helping them control their future spending. If a man knew in February that his cash income was $500 and his still unpaid bills from Christmas totalled $800, he would restrain himself from buying that electric saw he wanted. The emotional weight of the bills would be a powerful restriction on his compulsion to buy, a way of controlling his whims and desires, a very powerful brake. The third aspect of paying bills was that people needed to know the sequence and urgency of their bills. They knew how long the phone company would allow them to go without cutting off their phone, that the garbage people would wait six months before stopping collection, and they knew that the utility company would let them go up to 90 days without paying. Each bill has a certain length of time that it can go without being paid. So if one of the children ended up having a $600 dental bill and the dentist wouldn't do the rest of the work until he had a payment of $200, then the bill payer would make the $200 payment and reschedule the payment of all of his other bills. He was thus able, in effect, to borrow from his other creditors. If a relative died and he had to fly to Portland, he could leave with the full knowledge that the utility, gas, phone and garbage bills would wait. In essence, he would be able to get a two hundred dollar loan simply by manipulating the sequence in which he paid his bills.

What I found about paying bills, then, is that it's part of how people, including me, control themselves and their "hard to control desires." I have mentioned each of the ways that I found people use to pay their bills in the hope that in reading about them we can all become conscious of how we pay bills ourselves and consequently can all do a better job of it.

As I mentioned a few pages back, bills and loans are related. I think a strong argument can be given in favor of certain kinds of loans. One reason that I accept in my own daily life is that a loan can be a form of forced savings. Life insurance people validly argue that a good reason for having life insurance is that it's hard for people to save. Most people have rosy views of their future, and scaring them into buying life insurance is a way to help them force themselves to save.

Two years ago I borrowed $2,000 from a bank where I could get a low interest rate (because I was a former banker), put it into a savings and loan, and started paying it off on a monthly basis over a two year period. The net effect was that at the end of two years I had $2,000 in savings. It cost me only 2% per year to accomplish. (2% was the net difference of what I paid on the loan and the interest I received on the savings account.) I did this with the full knowledge that I was improving my credit standing for future emergencies. (Somewhere in the back of my mind I was telling myself that I had to be a good boy and make these payments, which I did.) That was forced savings. Essentially, a home mortgage or similar loan is much the same thing, a recognition that we need controls on our "desires."

Most of us seem to need limits. If you don't think you do then consider a test. See how easy it is for you to think of the next thing that you *want*. If you can spend three days and not think of the next thing that you want, you're right — you don't need self-imposed limits.

All this sort of middle class money discussion reminds me that not everyone fits the model; loans aren't really that universally appropriate. Jug 'n' Candle walks around the United States barefoot, wearing work pants, a Navy peajacket and a hat. He could go a long time without ever thinking of something that he wants, other than maybe a snort of cocaine, and it is highly doubtful that he would think of going into debt to get a supply of coke. However, if you want a new tape recorder, a Pakistani coin, or a new windmill for your communal water pump, restrictions are going to be necessary within your life and within your life-style.

As I have been writing this there has been a schism in my mind. On the one hand, I realize that nearly every reader has the problem of lack of money control—even an enormous percentage of people who really *think* they don't. On the other hand, there are a *few* people who really don't have needs and desires other than rudimentary ones. Those few include people willing to live anywhere, eat beans or rice or go three days without eating. Usually they devote their lives to something other than their personal whims. They range from a priest in a Zen center to a devoted revolutionary living in a basement, plotting the overthrow of the Santa Monica police. My advice has to be useful for both groups, the overwhelming majority and the exceptional few.

A very simple way to keep track of money is to have a checking account—something absolutely, unassailably essential for the vast majority of people. Even with the slightest effort you can find a bank that either doesn't charge you or requires a small minimum balance. I have heard the argument that "if I only use cash, I can't spend more than I earn." The logic is fine in the few instances where a person is earning $50.00 a week and spends it on grass and having a good time. However, in most instances where you have responsibilities it pays to have a checking account. It's a very simple way of keeping track of what you spend money on, which is an important part of the Second Law. It also creates a consciousness of your money-related behavior, putting it all in a sort of perspective.

There are two approaches that are useful in balancing your checkbook. One is to get two checking accounts—especially if they are cheap or free. Then one month you write checks out of one check book and the next month you write out of the other. What will happen is that leaving one account fallow will allow all the checks to clear, leaving your bank balance the same as your checkbook. Another approach is to *add* in your checkbook instead of subtracting. I discovered this from some ingenious suburban housewives. Say you deposit $160.00. Instead of subtracting the amount of each check, you simply enter the amount of the checks as you write them and total them until they reach $160.00. It's much easier to add than it is to subtract—and faster.

I'd like to talk about people, and the way we handle money. How the ethic of money permeates our lives.

I have a friend whom I call "130% Jack". One of Jack's

characteristics is that he always claims he can get you a deal, but whatever Jack's deal is you can be sure that it will cost 30% more than the normal retail price. Jack, however, actually believes that he's saving you money. Jack is well paid, spends an enormous amount of money on dope and is sort of muddle headed. He has a general belief that money will take care of itself, a kind of misreading of the First Law. It's a misreading because he violates the Second Law, which deals with our personal lives and which implies a sort of neatness, an ability to organize, a coherence. Ultimately, the money ethic deals with our responsibility for our own lives, although our dealing with the money ethic usually remains on the periphery of living, indicating a sort of sleepiness. I'm not objecting to this, or moralizing about it, but rather suggesting that paying attention to the details of our lives is part of understanding who we are, and part of growing. Our inattentiveness toward money is enough of a misperception of reality that it can lead us into trouble, in the same sense that any misperception of reality can lead to trouble.

Jack leads a sheltered life, with a soft job among friends. His operating reality is presently close enough to the reality in his own mind so that things are O.K. But, in general, most of the world requires a perception of reality which involves a much more careful attention to money. Jack's friends are tolerant, but in a lower income level he might be considered an unfair dealer and end up being stabbed. On another level, in the business world, he would be considered an untrustworthy person, with his 130% deals. Fortunately for Jack, he is living in a situation where reality and his perception of reality are close enough.

Salli asked a question, and my answer makes me sound like I have precognition. In reality it is mearly a simple reflection of the Second Law. She asked whether Jack had just accomodated his perceived reality to the reality in which he was living, a reality where there are a number of people who aren't too harsh on him because of his use of money. I replied that since Jack had recently learned to scuba dive but I didn't yet know the details of it, a real measure of whether he had a general misperception of operating reality was whether or not he would take dope before he dove. I didn't actually know whether he did or didn't. But the operating reality of scuba diving is such that you can't take drugs, or you are likely to drown. Salli immediately told me that only the day before she had heard that Jack had smoked hash before he dove and had almost drowned. That convinced me that the perceived reality reflected in his handling of money is only part of a pervasive view of the world around him. The handling of money deals with an ethic, and ethics permeate the entire thing that we call "personality."

Salli and I discussed the question of whether you can change someone like Jack, who has such a characteristic. I finally settled on the analogy of Alcoholics Anonymous, which I got from Gregory Bateson's book *Steps to an Ecology of Mind*. Bateson says that Alcoholics Anonymous works when a person finally accepts that for the rest of his life he is going to be an alcoholic. He has to operate from that position and never go near a drink. He has to realize that not even after five years of being off booze will he be less of an alcoholic, that there is no such thing as an intelligent alcoholic who can control himself. Only when he realizes that there's nothing he can do, can he survive.

Salli asked "What about embezzlers? Does time in jail cure them?" I said that it generally does, because they usually can't get a job again where they'll have a chance to embezzle. Then I remembered an exception—a friend of mine named Frank.

Frank was exactly what you'd expect an embezzler to be. He was a 26-year-old bachelor in San Diego who lived so high that I was always astounded. Frank was very open about describing how he had ingeniously arranged to shift his finances around. For example, he was on the loan committee of a savings and loan company. Because of his position on the loan committee, a bank that was affiliated with the savings and loan lent him enough money to buy a fancy Jaguar XKE. He was able to borrow on a 30-month payment plan with a balloon at the end (meaning that the bulk of the principal didn't have to be paid back until the end of the loan period). This is, of course, an extremely bad lending policy, because by the end of the 30-month period the value of the car would be negligible and the source of income to pay it off might not be around. It turned out that Frank was embezzling from his S & L by making loans to himself in the names of several customers. He was discovered when he left the country for a short vacation. He had a friend mail his monthly payments, but unfortunately for Frank his friend was six days late in sending in the money. Automatic notices went out from the computer to the people in whose names the loans were made. They came into the S & L very irate because they knew nothing about the loan. Frank was promptly caught.

Frank had what is known as chutzpah. After he was caught he tried to get himself sent to a nice minimum-security prison in Arizona, but, alas, the judge wasn't so nice, and he was sent to Terminal Island Prison in Los Angeles for one year. After Frank got out he couldn't get any job whatsoever, since he had been trained only as a banker and now had an embezzlement conviction and jail term behind him. He was at his wits' end for more than a year. He might well have ended up a circus barker if it weren't for the fact that he came to an unusual self-understanding. He ran an ad in the **Wall Street Journal** which read FORMER EMBEZZLER AVAILABLE FOR WORK. In the ad he briefly explained his background and what he went to jail for. He got over thirty responses to his ad. I would tend to agree with most of the people who attempted to hire him—somebody who fully recognizes what he had done is capable of controlling his future behavior.

Frank turned out to be quite successful. Within a year he was living very well on the Spanish Riviera—as the result of a good salary, his reward for being a competent financier.

In addition to the rule that you must keep track of your money, it's important to know who you are and where you are in money terms. This comes out most clearly when you apply for a loan—although it applies less to individuals than to projects and businesses.

One of the first things I do when I'm acting as a financial consultant for a client is to get him to the point where he is eligible for a bank loan. I recommend this also for non-profit bodies, sometimes encouraging *part* of a non-profit organization to apply for a loan, often collateralized by the rest of the organization. Now why do I do this? Because the whole process of getting a loan is a powerful way of getting insight into what your business or project is. Bankers are generally clear-sighted, narrow and unimaginative, which is fine, since the bank's purpose is to make 100% secured loans without taking any risks whatsoever. Risk-taking in banking is incompetence. If you feel that banks should take risks with their money then you probably have a misconception of what the function of a bank is. Banks do lend to many other institutions like finance companies, retail stores and others which *are* in the business of taking risks with their loanable funds. But the bank is the wholesaler and tries to have zero risk. In fact, any time a bank gets much above 3/10ths of 1% loss in its general lending it is being poorly operated, and this is pretty close to being no loss at all.

What are we doing, then, when we take someone to a bank? We are saying that he or she has enough perception of the money reality in which he operates to be able to say something about his future, with virtually no risk implied. In order to say something that strong about the future, people have to have a pretty accurate perception of themselves.

In the case of my private clients, once they have this self-perception I make it clear that the first thing to do is get to know the loan officer at the bank, and this involves time. Usually it takes as much as a year for a banker to get to know you.

What do you do when you go to the bank for a loan? You prepare three things: a general financial statement, a projection, and a personal financial statement.

(1) A general financial statement applies to a business or a project. You might want one for your personal money keeping practices. It's an accurate record of what you have done up to date. It includes a balance sheet and an income and expense statement.

It would be easy to show you a picture of a balance sheet or an income-expense statement, but if I put one in the book most people flipping through the pages would be scared shitless and never read it. So I'll try to describe one with words. (If you actually have to do one, get a book with a picture of one in it.)

The balance sheet generally has three sections: assets, liabilities and net worth.

a) Assets are cash in the bank on the day of the statement, money people owe you, and the value of physical things such as a building or an inventory. They are usually listed in descending order from the most liquid to the least liquid—liquid meaning how fast an item can be turned into cash. For example, collecting a debt of $200 might take a month, but selling your chicken coop for cash might take five years.

(b) Liabilities are what you owe. They, too, are listed in descending order—from the most pressing item needing to be paid to the least pressing. Under liabilities comes your phone bill and rent, the accumulated payroll to the date of the statement, what you owe the bank, and last of all the loan you promised to repay your cousin if the project succeeds.

(c) Net worth is what you get if you subtract what you owe (liabilities) from your assets. It can be negative in some cases.

An income-expense statement is just that. At the top is listed your income over the last period of time (a month, quarter, or year); below that are your expenses for the same period. At the bottom is the difference between expense and income, either a surplus or a deficit. Income is the total money that came in. Expenses are everything that you wrote checks for, including payroll, business trips to Mazatlan, and the clay urn at the front door that you bought on your trip. A balance sheet is a snapshot of you, your project or your business at *one* point in time; it's just as if you should empty your pockets and count what's in them, figure out the value of your sweater, shoes and Swiss army knife and write it all down on a piece of paper. An income-expense statement is a history of what happened.

What is a balance sheet for? Anything— profit making, a non-profit venture, even a picture of your personality and behavior can be put on a balance sheet. It's a way of letting a banker know, in clear terms, what you've done. By studying the structure of your financial statements he can ask intelligent questions and get even more information. That is exactly what a banker is trained to do—to look at ratios, the relationship between money in one part of your statement and money in some other part. This simply leads him to ask logical questions, and from seeing a certain ratio he'll ask the same question of the Memorex Company, which is hundreds of millions of dollars in debt, that he'll ask of you.

(2) The second thing you need is a projection. A projection is usually an estimate of future income and expenses. In most cases it is simply a straight-line forecast of the future based on past experience. Although it is simple it is very significant. To be able to project what is going to happen means that you have an understanding of your existing reality. That is why it is valuable to get people to go to a bank for a loan—because they are required to make a projection, which in turn requires the examination of themselves in enough detail to be able to understand their operating reality.

Let me give you an example of what I do with the clients I work with and their projects. We sit down together and make a projection. We work together because as an outsider I can look at their future more objectively than they can, not being as optimistic as they are in hoping for good revenues or in thinking that they can keep expenses from going up. The result is that I am able to help them look more closely at their present situation, to give them a better sense of their capabilities and of what they are doing. This helps them to face what their activities are realistically and to confront their operating reality. Being forced to make projections requires them to get an overall view of the interacting forces within their organization. The projection is particularly powerful because it requires an understanding of some of the major forces involved in the business.

The really surprising thing about a projection is that it is extremely simple. Once you have made one or two you will be amazed at how simple it is to do and yet how powerful it can be in affecting your understanding.

Let's start with the simplest way to do one. Take your past growth rate, sales and expenses, and assume that this rate will be the same for the coming period—let's say a year.

Suppose you grew from last year to this year by 20% in revenues and 18% in expenses. Simply project these percentages for the coming year and break them down so that for each month you get equal increases in revenue and expenses. Now, this is unrealistic because you know that revenues and expenses vary on a month by month basis, so go back and look at your seasonal patterns. Did you do better in August? Is November a bad month? This process can be a powerful eye-opener. A number of my clients became conscious for the first time that there was a pattern that business was bad in September and October, for example, and extremely good in November and December. They may have known this intuitively but they had not actually seen the consequences of these fluctuations on paper. A strong awareness of their situation made it possible for them to borrow from the bank well in advance of their need and to pay back their loan promptly. This helped to establish extremely good relations with the bank because it indicated that they understood their business and had enough vision to enable them to anticipate problems. Understanding the cyclic patterns of revenues and expenses can make a big difference.

Sometimes when you look at expenses you feel a little uneasy about some that seem high or others that look too low. This is a signal to go back to see what the relationships are. You might find that when revenues go up in March, labor costs go up in May. You are now forced to look at some of the interrelationships in your business. In many companies these may not be so obvious (they may well be intutitive), but as you look at them you will find patterns that are important in understanding what to do.

In making projections I have often been extraordinarily accurate in predicting both revenues and expenses—sometimes within 1% or 2% per month. Clients have been baffled by this, and I smile enigmatically. The fact is that any fairly good projection in a situation where conditions are pretty stable will be surprisingly accurate. I think you've got the point.

(3) The third thing you prepare for the bank is a personal financial statement. This is a very useful thing for most people, because in many situations there is an intricate rela-

tionship between the principal individual and the project or business. In reality they are integrated, although legally they are separated. Looking at a personal balance sheet gives a person a significantly better understanding of who he is and how much he is devoting to his project or his business, and essentially what his life-time commitment is. Is he paying himself a lot and putting very little back? Is he increasing his personal worth in terms of cars and houses, or is he depleting his savings and building up the market value of his company? A personal financial statement is a useful tool because it confronts you visually with what the banker will be looking for. He wants to see what the relationship is between you and your commitment, your energy and your passion.

It's worthwhile making a personal financial statement periodically. I suggest you make a copy of each statement so you can go back and make comparisons with each new one.

Taking all these things to the bank is probably one of the most powerful exercises in personal growth; its power is magnified when one realizes that a relationship with the bank is something that extends over a period of time. The concrete value of a "projection sheet" is being able to show someone else (the bank) that you have goals and visions and that you are able to relate to them over a period of time. It is a way of saying that your perceived reality and your operating reality are pretty close to each other in terms of money. It's also a demonstration to the banker that you are capable of judging yourself, and judging yourself fairly accurately.

I'll use some specific examples of my clients and what happened in their relationships with the banks. In the first case Sal, at the time I became his advisor was in extremely bad shape financially, heavily in debt to the bank (very poor sales revenue) and with all bills more than 90 days past due. By helping him prepare the kinds of materials that the banker now required I was able to help him understand his business realistically and to give him a sense of what was economically feasible. I also helped him to understand what had to be done, how much sales he had to generate, and to what extent he had to work late and on weekends to keep his actual out-of-pocket labor costs from driving him out of business.

We went to the bank, and the banker was very impressed with our careful analysis. The bank had at least two choices. It could demand full payment of the loan at that time and put Sal out of business (both he and the bank would have lost in that case), or it could try to find some solution that would allow Sal to stay in business. Now remember that the bank could have closed Sal's business down in hopes of getting some of the assets which were there. Banks are usually the first ones in line when it comes to dividing up the property of a creditor. But in this case the bank agreed to reduce the amount of each payment required to repay Sal's loan.

Sal also did something that he had never done before. He started paying by check, delivering it to the banker in person on the day it was due—or sometimes even a day before. He did this for six months, giving absolute, utter priority to this responsibility, paying the bank before he paid all other bills— including his own salary. At the end of the six months we had not only achieved the goals set out in the financial projection but the banker was so personally satisfied with the delivery of payments that he willingly extended the payment schedule for the balance, allowing Sal to accumulate enough money to bring all other back debts current. This was no friendly country banker who reacted so well, incidentally; it was the Bank of America. Within seven months after I had become Sal's financial advisor he was relatively debt free.

My second client's experience was similar, but in his case he needed to get a bank loan, not to pay one off. At the time I took him on as a client Sheldon was well beyond the point of bankruptcy, although none of his creditors knew it. He had a great deal of money coming in, but he was past due in paying nearly all his bills. He was living on borrowed time, capitalizing his company on his creditors' money. Sheldon didn't have any personal resources left, having already poured them into the company to get it started. His company had a relatively large swing in sales revenue. On top of this, as more business came in more capital was needed to cover labor costs until the revenue from the sale of products was received—a fairly typical growth business problem.

Since investors, his only possible source of money, were unlikely to help because the firm was in an unglamorous and highly specialized field, he could only turn to a bank.

The first year that I worked with Sheldon's company we sent all his financial statements to local banks, indicating a desire for a bank loan. He was treated as coldly as anyone could conceivably be. In most cases the banks said, "Very nice to meet you. Hope to see you again. Let us know if we can ever be of any help." One year later, however, through simple, careful attention to the books and careful control of expenses (with regular planning sessions about sales), the company made a miraculous turnaround. We went back to the banks, this time with new financial statements, and, although the reader probably won't believe this, the bankers literally hugged my client. They were so impressed with the change in financial conditions that they asked for the opportunity to make a loan. One of the banks ended up by offering to make an unsecured loan for a substantial amount any time Sheldon needed one. Today Sheldon knows how to use this line of credit, and he uses it frequently. He has been able to expand his business without outside capital and to maintain complete control of his own company. He can grow on borrowed bank money, as he well deserves, because of the amount of time and energy he has put into the firm so far. The lesson of this is that his financial figures and his relationship with the bank were very important. The bank lending relationship requires an understanding of yourself and an accurate enough picture of reality to allow you to operate effectively.

Salli Rasberry asks about three terms: capitalization, investor and unsecured loan. I'm not much for definitions, but in each of these terms there is a pretty straight-forward concept. Interestingly, these concepts are the same everywhere, from Ulan Bator, Mongolia to Kiev to Naples to Alamogordo, New Mexico.

Capitalization is the core money that a business or an individual has to fall back upon for either emergencies or for business expansion. For example, you are producing about $400 worth of special sandals in a rural community in Arizona. You buy your leather for $200. The money you receive in sales is more than enough to allow you to buy next month's leather. The orders you get are not so great that you couldn't double your shoe production if you wanted to, because you've got enough leather on hand and can wait the extra month it takes for all the letters with payment to come back. Everything is running smoothly when all of a sudden an article about your sandals appears in *The Whole Earth Catalog*. Your orders, instead of being $400 worth a month, jump to $15,000 a month. The leather you need now would cost you $6,000 but you have only $400 in the bank. So you're stuck. There aren't going to be any bankers around your part of the country who will know how reliable those thousands of *Whole Earth* readers are who have placed orders for your shoes. They will probably be unwilling to advance you the money because they don't know you; you've never been in their bank and you don't have an account there. There's almost no chance that you are going to be able to do anything but send out mimeographed letters to all the people who ordered sandals saying, "I'm sorry we can't produce your shoes unless you want to send us some money in advance." Since very few people will actually be willing to do that, you're in trouble. The money that you need is for capitalization—money for expansion. In this case it's the money you use to finance other people's credit.

Another example would be where your shoe business is humming along beautifully, producing $15,000 worth of sandals a month, when one of your major buyers, a department store in Los Angeles that buys $5,000 worth a month, starts having financial trouble and is now paying 50 to 60 days late. You know the rest of your sales will continue, but if your labor costs and your leather costs can't be cut down, or your sales to the department store stopped, you might go out of business. Once again, the bank doesn't know you and doesn't know the Los Angeles department store. It is theoretically possible that on some written guarantee from the department store, if its credit was extremely good—and if the bank knew you—the bank would lend you the money. (This is the reason to get to know your banker; banks make loans mostly to people they know.) The money you need for the one or two months in order to continue payments for leather and labor while awaiting payment from the department store would have to come from somewhere. This is why you need capital, to serve as a reserve for just such an emergency.

Another concept Salli asked about is *investor*. In general, an investor is somebody who puts up money in return for future income. Anyone can be an investor, whether he has no net worth or a lot of wealth. There is no special amount of money that makes one an investor. In Japan an investor is often a member of a large syndicate of people from different walks of life who all put equal amounts of money into a large investment pool. In South Africa an investor can be a laborer who joins other laborers who migrate to work for six months, all of them pooling their wages in order to purchase a small business upon their return.

The concept of an investor is different from that of a lender. A lender gives you his money, and after a certain period of time he gets all of it back with interest in addition. There is an explicit, if not written agreement that the money loaned is not being risked and that there will be interest paid for its use. An investor, on the other hand, takes the same risks as the individual who is directly responsible for the enterprise he invests in. He will gain back in proportion to the amount of risk that he has assumed.

An acquaintance of mine makes an illegal little device that you put on your telephone so a person calling you won't get billed for his call. He can build the units for $10 apiece and sells them for $40. When he produces forty, for a total gross revenue of $1600, he just about covers all of his expenses, including labor.

When he got started he needed $400 to buy the electronic components. There were two ways he could have gotten it—he could either have found an investor or have borrowed the money. If he had had to borrow it he would have had to take a bank loan at 5% interest for a year, which means that on the $400 he would only have had to pay back $420 after a year. Well, he doesn't deal with bankers, so he had to borrow four hundred dollars for two months and pay back $450. Such a loan had to be from someone who knew and trusted him, the $50 fee compensating for his friend's inconvenience.

An investor, on the other hand, is someone who would have said "Look, I'll give you the $400, but I want to share in your profit. You'll be getting $1,200 out of this product. A lot of it goes to reward you for your time, but a lot of it repays you for the risk you take in doing an illegal thing. For my four hundred dollars I'll take the risk along with you, one of the risks being that the phone company might develop a way to detect your devices and after that no one would want to buy any more. One other risk is that you might get arrested. Because of this I want 10% of your net return after cost." That would be 10% of $1,200, which would be a return of $120 on his $400 if everything went well.

In the case of the person who receives a *loan* there is an implied responsibility. If this aquaintence who makes the telephone gadgets is honest, he'd spend a lot of time over the next six or eight months repaying his lender even if the deal fell through. Even if he went to jail he'd be obligated to repay the loan as soon as he got out.

Finally, loans fall into the category of either "secured" or "unsecured." In case of a secured loan the lender has a specific object in mind that the borrower will have to sell to make up for the loan in case he can't repay it. A pawn shop deals in secured loans—but here there is a highly unusual relationship between the price of the merchandise and the amount of the loan. For example, you could take a $600 typewriter to a pawn broker but you might be able to borrow only $50 on it—a pretty bad ratio. At a bank, however, a $3,000 car generally entitles you to borrow $2,000 assuming that you have insurance to make sure the car is repaired if it is ever damaged.

A credit card account is an example of an unsecured loan. If you can't repay the debt you create, the credit card company has no specific thing of yours to sell, so they will try to raise the money by attaching your wages or in other ways, which can involve the courts, bankruptcy, etc. Because there's generally more risk involved in a loan that is unsecured the lender usually charges more interest. If one of the businesses described a few pages back should go into bankruptcy, an outstanding (still unpaid) secured loan would give the bank greater rights over the property to be liquidated than an unsecured loan would.

While we are at it, here are two other concepts which many people balk at or grow up failing to comprehend: "gross" and "net." Gross has a pretty standard meaning. It's the final price in a production chain of a product or service. An example: the price of this book as sold over the counter is its gross price. If you want to know gross receipts for the sale of the book, it would be the number of books sold times that price. Suppose we sold 100,000 paperback books at $3.95 each, then $395,000 would be the gross revenue on this book.

The same is true of any item. Gross is the largest number relating to the amount of the sale. From the gross amount other expenses or other percentages are subtracted, leaving the "net." Anything less than the gross is a net. So if somebody talks about a net you have to find out what net he means. Net has no specific meaning. For example, the net percentage the publisher might expect to get on this book is 10%, which is 10% of the retail gross price, $3.95. Someone else might be talking about the net of something else—say the net of what the bookseller pays the publisher for the book. He may pay only $2.16 for the book, so if somebody was talking about 10% of *that* net figure it would be substantially different than 10% of the gross. If you hear the term net, find out what it refers to. If you hear the term gross, you don't have to be told what it is.

Accounting is a field in which technical words usually have a sound reason for their existence: they are shorthand for concepts that are regularly used. (This is unlike medicine where terminology is often used to mystify the public. Lately, a large number of women have been trying to understand enough about medicine to de-mystify it and develop a terminology that is easy to understand. I see no such pattern developing in the monetary field.) Actually, very few words in the acounting or economics field are designed to be mystifying or obscure; you simply have to learn the concepts so that you can use them.

Before I close this chapter there are a few bits of Ann Landers-type advice that I would like to add.

When you open a checking account, open it with the largest amount of money you possibly can. I'm not kidding! Even if the average balance in your account is only going to be $50, try to borrow a friend's $10,000 (home down payment) for *one day* so you can use it to open your account. You don't have to go that far, but anything over a couple of thousand dollars looks good. You can withdraw most of the money a few days after the account is opened. Really! The reason for this is that the bank records your opening balance on your signature card (and often in other places, too), believing that it is representative of your financial status. I did a study when I was a banker and found absolutely no correlation between opening balances and the kind of balances that appeared later on in the same account. It's such a strong tradition to do it this way (at least a hundred years old) that bankers still judge people by their opening balance. Try it; the branch manager will smile on you forever more.

It may seem middle class to have credit, but if you have it you need less money. "Credit" is the ability to borrow, and if your credit is good you don't need savings—or at least you need less savings. Savings are generally for emergencies, but if you have credit you can use it in an emergency instead of your savings, and pay it back later. For example, if you're busted in Marrakech and a $500 bribe will get you out, you can get an "advance" on your American Express card.

All it takes to establish credit is a little time and a little stability. You need *one* job, one address, a phone and a checking account for one year. Having decided to establish a good credit rating and already having a job and an address, wait four months and then apply for a gasoline credit card. Next apply for credit at a luxury store (they give credit *very* readily because their losses on credit are covered by the high mark-up on their merchandise). After six months apply at Sears or Macy's or a similar middle-price-range national store. Their credit is the very hardest to get and can really get you the rest. Use these credit accounts once or twice and pay promptly. After from seven to nine months you can apply for Master Charge or Bankamericard (not both at the same time). When you get them your credit is really established (after a few months, you can ask by letter to have your credit card borrowing amount raised). Now you are free—you can get a new job as often as you wish and move as often as you feel like it; your credit is established. Just remember to pay your accounts promptly, and never have a run-in with a jewelry store! Most bad credit ratings are put in the credit rating computers by jewelry stores—the $300-diamond-studded-watch-type places.

Credit is dependent mostly on stability. Your stability is measured by the time you stay with a job (they check), the time you have lived at your present and previous residence, whether or not you have a phone (bad debtors usually avoid having their own phone), and by your checking account. Be sure not to overdraw your checking account more than once or twice a year: sometimes your bank may keep track of it, and sometimes the word gets around to other banks.

Lastly, if you need a loan, shop around. The bigger the loan, the more important this is. Banks are not monolithic; each branch is different. Some have loan officers or managers who are liberal, smart and understanding; others have insensitive bores who retired at age twenty-four when they joined the bank. Ask around. If you need a loan for a specialized purpose—say an organic restaurant or to import merchandise from Zanzibar—find someone who got a similar loan and go to their lender. Specialized knowledge and good experience on past loans are what encourage a lender to make additional loans in esoteric areas.

Jug

A Story

It began like this:
             'I have a canoe.'
             'I have two!'

In truth, no two canoes were alike in those days and two canoes close enough alike to be EQUAL were VALUED as a magic happening. Therefore, when the People heard of his two canoes, they took the canoes from him and enshrined them so that he had to build himself a third canoe, and it was definitely different.

Many winters passed. In time, however, ideas of equivalence (EQUAL VALUE) circulated in the Mind of the people and new ways unfolded:

  1) restitution and payment

  2) accounting

  3) mass production (equivalence)

To live with money means to live with the three ways. The flow of money around and through the three ways is like the flow of conversation around and through life. As words are not things
So money never makes it right.

As plans are not doing
So money by itself is never enough.

If you say something twice and do not mean it, you make yourself a slave to the Word
If you add meaning to what you say every time you say it, the Word is your ally.

So
   think
           this
                way

Look at your coin, look at your folding money, pay attention to it, treat it like works of art, it is, no mistake, some of the best printer's work for the Treasury.

The stories mellowed-out old silver dollars can tell! Treat them like friends.
           Don't try to possess it.
           (Remember the Hope Diamond.)
           Lest it possess you!

58

Charlotte

Charlotte Mayerson, my very wise editor with Random House, asked me for a *positive* illustration for keeping good records of money. The obvious one is a matter of being able to know that you are in control of yourself, the plain old "security of the womb" feeling.

It sure can help in personal and family relations! Sharon Daniels and I have found that we have had occasional money related arguments over the three years we have lived together. The arguments seem to come about twice a year over who is paying more than their fair share of expenses. After we recognize the nature of the argument, we sit down with our separate checkbooks and piles of receipts and figure out what we've earned and what we've spent; (it's always a shock to find out where all that money went) and we make whatever adjustments are necessary.

The resulting calm and love are *positive*!

THE
THIRD LAW

MONEY IS A DREAM: A Fantasy
As Alluring As The Pied Piper

Money is very much a state of mind. It's much like the states of consciousness that you see on an acid trip. Maybe it is the animal figure seen in the peyote dream (Mescalito). It is fantasy in itself, purely a dream. People who go after it as though it were real and tangible, say a person who is trying to earn a hundred thousand dollars, orients their life and ends up in such a way as to have been significantly changed simply to reach that goal. They become part of that object and since the object is a dream (a mirage) they become quite different from what they set out to be.

To really understand the extent to which money is a dream listen to the economist's definition of money, it is: *part of a system of relative pricing and an accounting store of value.* Let's take the second, a store of value. It is a record of previous transactions like your savings account, your checking account. These records are an indication of credits of labor, credits of energy or inheritance that you have built up. It is a store of imaginary value. When you think in terms of it as part of a relative pricing system the fantasy element becomes even more dramatic. In theoretical terms, the price of anything in this world is determined by the demand of everybody else in the world for that item in proportion to its scarcity. Money is the communication medium that records these pressures throughout the world. The abstract reason a pair of nylons costs $2.25 is because that is the relative demand for a particular pair of nylons, in *a* store (Macy's on May 15) in comparison to the needs of all the people in the world and available resources of

61

those people relative to the other available resource demands for the production of those stockings. You can see from even the vaguest description of what money is that it must be a dream.

I hope you can realize that people who set goals that are related to money, are bound to follow a peculiar road the same way that someone in real life sets out to find the animal he or she saw on their last mescaline trip must inevitably stumble and bump into things and realize in the end that they have become something of a fantasy themselves in the search.

SALLY: Can you clarify that?

Say you've got the $100,000 that you desired. You are now the process that it took you to get there. If you had to sell dope, you're a dope dealer with $100,000. You don't just have $100,000. Because by then you're the shrewd dope dealer, or you're the tough president of a junkyard, that's what you are. All of a sudden the dream has disappeared. You're striving for something that's totally a dream and how can you be a dream. If you were searching for a piece of 11th century sculpture that you wanted for your front yard (which is similar to but still quite different from having $50,000 dollars in the front yard) in the process you'd become a collector, part of that sculpture, you'd grow because of it—because of the search. But when you set out for a dream, you become a dream yourself, you're something you never thought you'd be and nobody wants you except those people who are in your dream. If you're the really bright young Harvard student who's interested in everything, including making a million dollars, then likely you will end up in Peoria, Illinois running a junkyard and have a million dollars. You will have only the people who appreciate your million dollars, and peers in the junk business as friends and their only concern is what's happening to the price of steel. You won't even read the front page of the Wall Street Journal—you'd just to turn to page 27 every day to check the stock prices.

COMMENTARY ON THE THIRD LAW

I think you might be interested in knowing that this book was originally transcribed from a tape recorded conversation between Salli and me—actually a monologue with periodic questions. For some reason, the original taping of the third law section was erased. In doing it over Salli and I spent a lot of time trying to remember what I said. Maybe that says something about the fact that money is a dream—it evaporated from our tape.

The money that man uses everywhere in the world is the same. The yen, the pound, the dollar, the peso are all manipulated and function in the same way. The governments of the world try to regulate their supplies of money, and they all use similar theories. Money is one thing that we all have in common; it's a dream, an illusion, it's not real. *It is a relationship between all things in the world.* Just hearing myself say that reminds me of its dreamlike qualities.

I want to examine this dreamlike quality of money before I try to describe what happens to people who deal with it. Dreams have a number of qualities that relate to money. A dream is not something that can be placed in the past or the future. It is always immediate and present. A dream does things, as Gregory Bateson points out in *Steps to an Ecology of Mind;* it cannot be a negative. In a dream you don't say I am *not* going to the store. The dream acts out the negative and carries it to its conclusion, either absurd or fatal. For example, you go to the store, and a giant artichoke eats you.

Money doesn't have a past or a future, except in a very abstract way. Take, for example, your net worth, which is something you have accumulated over time. It may include something your parents accumulated, yet there's no particular piece of currencey which embodies that time span. All you have is an abstract symbol of some events that occurred in the past; The money itself doesn't have attributes of the past. Money is always the present; it embodies no concept of future.

Economists over the past twenty years have come to

realize that we cannot borrow from the future. Governments used to be accused of borrowing from future generations when they incurred enormous war debts; it was argued that future children would have to pay off those debts. It's now clear to economists that there is no way to borrow from the future. The only wealth that exists is that which is currently available from the combination of labor, energy, tools and resources. You just cannot make future people or future resources available at the present, so money has the dream quality of having no future.

Let's have a look at money's lack of "negativeness". Money is nearly always related to action. We exchange things, we come to some sort of agreed price on the relative values of the things we exchange—and that's money (at least that's the price component of money). A debt, or negative net worth, is not really negative; it's just a direction of flow—from debtor to creditor. There's essentially no way to do something with money that is the equivalent of saying "Don't go to the store". (This is hard to grasp; it's a Zen koan like "not does not exist.") Money is just there. Similarly, you can't say something has no value, which would mean that it has no exchange price. Everything has an exchange value; somebody somewhere would want it at some sufficiently low price. My typing table doesn't have an innate value, but it does have a value in exchange. I can't make that value disappear by just saying it's going to disappear. On the other hand, I can only make it exist at the time I am going to exchange it.

Economists would point out that somethings are treated as free—with no price—but they aren't. Air and ocean have been conventionally viewed tht way. Of course, we are now paying for our idea that the air is free in the form of medical costs for lung cancer, auto pollution controls, and in countless other ways. We are paying higher prices for fish and working to clean our beaches because of our treatment of the ocean as a free thing.

To add to the picture of money as a dream, look at its universality. It's the same in Zanzibar, Montreal, Bogalusa and Peru. Everywhere that man is he has price, capital, wholesale, retail, interest, profit, tax, cash vs. accrual, inflation and deflation. Something as complex as that is everywhere we are; only language seems to be as universal a human trait. Look at each word and how dreamlike it is—for example, inflation. Our government, 2000 miles away from me, writes checks for more dollars than it receives in taxes and the money I have in my pocket decreases in value; it now costs me more to buy nearly everything.

I hope that all these rambling words can somehow convey to you that money is a dream. What might all this mean? If your chase after a dream, you will have a grasping clenched fist in the end and a sore hand with nothing in it. In a sense that's what happens to the kind of person who spends all his life seeking money. He's seeking something that is unreal, that doesn't exist, and what he will end up with is a hollow existence. In the end he is not the same person he started out to be. Maybe someone can convince me otherwise by introducing me to a person whose goal was to make a lot of money and who ended up a whole and interesting person, but my experience with people who set out to make a lot of money is that when they get it they find there's very little they can do with it, or they have changed so much they are not at all what they wanted to be.

One of my close friends is an example of the fist clenching—money type whose fist is now empty. I've known Melissa for eleven years. I met her when she first opened her own art gallery. It was an excellent gallery and she was a first rate painter. She was a bright, happy, warm person who was loved by many and who had become the center of an exciting circle of friends. As she learned the gallery business she found that she was good at sales and very good at her business. It grew, and her little spark of interest in getting enough money to run a nice gallery became a flaming passion for big business. She is earning lots of money now—her business has expanded beyond the art gallery but she is a different person. I no longer feel comfortable around her. She talks about her fancy sports car, her home in the country, her foreign buying trips, and mostly about how well her business is doing. She's not very happy. She has few friends, narrow interests; she goes through men like a hurricane through a corn field. She rarely paints anymore, and she works long hours at money making. I stayed with her for a while recently and saw what a lonely person she has become and what a tyrant she is with her employees.

Another person worth describing used to be a close friend of Sharon's, the woman I live with. Her name is Judy. She and Sharon were close friends. Judy was a hard working, warm woman from an upper-middle-class background. Somewhere along the line she decided she wanted to become rich, and for her that meant a rich lover. She found one, and, now she lives in villas around the world, buys new dresses for every big party and is au courant on all the latest fads of the jet set. We find her difficult to be with. She can talk about little else but butlers, maids and the problems of wealth, and she doesn't like the man she lives with.

These sound like stereotypes but they're not. Nor are the people in such situations necessarily unhappy. What happens, though, is that their worship of money changes them to such an extent that the quest for money becomes their whole life.

Salli asked about the positive aspect of dreams and fantasy. I think it is the realization that a fantasy can stretch your priorities. Fantasy is a way of challenging your own conventional and immediate value structure. For instance, people often talk to me about having a piece of land where they can go to get away from it all and live peacefully. I can show these people how they can get their land in less than a year. They will have to sacrifice a number of things in order to be able to get it, but suggesting that they strive for their fantasy will lead to an examination of their priorities. The same applies to almost anything. An 18 year old woman was telling me last week that she wanted a new ElDorado. I could have told her how she could get an ElDorado by not buying any new dresses for a year, by working an extra three hours a week and maybe by doing some "Avon calling" on Wednesday evenings. That kind of fantasy, realistically examined, would force her to ask herself about her other priorities—such as how important a new dress is to her, or how important is living in a $160 apartment compared to living with three other people and spending only $40 a month.

In most cases, no change in the availability of money is going to change a person's priorities. People usually know what they want to do, but they're unwilling to acknowledge whatever it is within their personality that makes them do what they're doing and leads to their self deception. It is certainly not money that puts them where they are. People invariably have scapegoats, and money has always been one of the most convenient ones—because it is commonly agreed that we can't do most of the things we want to do because we don't have enough money. As long as the majority of us believe that, it may be a useful, convenient mirage. Unfortunately in some other cultures it's been the Jews who supposedly kept things from happening, and thus people (The Germans and Poles, for example) set out to kill the Jews. I think the money scapegoat might be a little better one for a culture to believe in, because it's pretty hard to kill money (although that's what a lot of barter freaks have suggested should be done.)

Later on, under Laws Five and Six, I'll tell about my experiences in giving. At this point, however, to emphasize that money is a dream-thing, I'd like to relate one of the most powerful experiences I gained from being on the Board of POINT and having a few thousand dollars to spend with no restrictions. The Board deliberately made unrestricted money available to all Board members in order to find out what it would do to us. I have come to realize that nothing I had ever wanted to do had been prevented because of lack of money. What I did with the POINT money however, was to accelerate actually doing some of the things I had wanted to do, which let me get out of my system a couple of the things that proved to be trivial. (Until they were done, however, I didn't realize that they were trivial.)

For example, the money allowed me to build some sex furniture—therapeutic furniture—so that people could have sex in more positions than are possible by just lying on a flat bed. I had been thinking about this furniture for nine years. Finally, when I built the furniture I found that nobody wanted to use it. The availability of the money—in this case about $300—allowed my fantasy to become a reality, and something that had essentially been operating as a bottleneck in my mind was dispensed with. I had always had $300, which I could have spent on this project; it was just that I never used it. The idea was like a mental loop that kept going around and around, slowing me down on other things and affecting my development, a minor thing on my mind's back burner that had kept me from doing other major things. The access to money, to be able to do anything I wanted, didn't change my plans or my reality significantly. It did make me realize that money does not play a role in setting personal goals or in evaluating the world around you. Having access to money for any purpose helps to get some of the cobwebs out of the way. To get rid of all those cobwebs probably didn't cost more than $2,000, money which in the past I had occasionally had in savings.

Interestingly, one of the things that I had considered to be relatively minor—carving a mile-long sign in the desert with a tractor for observation by satellites—taught me a whole new lesson. In the struggle to get the project done I learned about how important a sense of "adventure" is. In carrying out the project I used heavy equipment and flying, and there were some risks and dangers involved. Almost all of my skills—as a pilot, a mathematician, a planner, a scientist, a friend, and a mystic—were required for this project. The whole thing gave me a taste of adventure, and it was spectacular, for I learned the importance of adventure in everyday life and how devastating the absence of it can be in creating boredom. Another thing I learned from the project was that some of my concepts weren't really as outrageous as I'd thought. I came to view it later as conceptual art and not just as a social consciousness project. From my desert sign adventure, close ties with a number of important conceptual artists developed, and new ideas in conceptual art evolved.

Now this was a small project (it cost $800), but in many ways the stumbling block aspect of it was such that I had to get it out of the way, and in the process of getting it out of the way I learned a great deal more about myself.

Having access to POINT Foundation money was like waking up from a dream. It takes very little to wake up from a dream, to realize the difference between a dream state and reality. If only everybody could live out the fantasy of having a million dollars, we might see a radically different world. If we could just begin to operate on that basis it could have significant effects on our lives.

The Next Time You Visit A Bank

Just walk into any bank, whether you're known there or not, go to the center of the lobby, keeping your hands at your side, stop, take about two minutes to turn around slowly and look at everything. Now, how do you feel? I'd be surprised if you would have feelings that strong even in a church. A bank is a modern day sacred place, and it evokes very strong culturally-ingrained reactions. Three things from my experience illustrate this.

First, as a banker I occasionally had reason to visit branch offices, sometimes taking friends with me. I would go behind the teller line for some reason, simply lifting the latch (I've never seen one that was secured by anything more than a simple latch) and walk through. My guests, however, wouldn't go near the back of the teller line; it was a taboo area. I could never even get them to put their little toe across.

Second, no promotion, scheme or display attracts attention when placed in a lobby. Paintings on display never sell, unless they are hanging near the loan officers desks where people sitting down have a chance to look at them. Even a TV set turned on during the World Series doesn't attract attention, unless it's in a window so people can see it from outside or in a corner far away from the bank transaction area.

Third and finally, a sociologist, Jane Prather, worked with me on a project where she was employed as a teller for three months. Jane noticed that within twelve feet of the bank entrance 95% of the customers would act in some way to show that they had a reason for being in the bank—like taking a pen out of a purse or reaching into a pocket for a wallet. And, of course, while waiting in line people almost never looked anywhere except straight ahead. Maybe we're all crooks and feel guilty about being in a bank.

Yeh, a bank is a strange place.

Jack O. Diamonds

You can
talk about your Casey Jones,
talk about your Frankie Lee,
your John Henry Steeldriver,
and, yes, you can talk about

your
         Stag
                 O
                       Lee

   Because however fast or slow your man may
be, he's nothin'
   compared . . . what I'm talkin' about . . . by the
name of
       Jack O. Diamonds . . . was a
       Double-Your-Money-Back Man.
Don't pay attention
   to everything you hear—
   Jack WAS born, as
   any man, of a

      storm
         pitch
            sea
and his Mama took
and hid him praying

"Lord, take him by the hand"

and the flood came
          and took him
                   in
                     to
                       land.

Give him to the Giver
Float him out to sea
Swim
    baby on the sand
and take him
      by
        the
          hand . . .

that's how
                they
                        almost
                                come to talk
of
        Jack O. Diamonds
                a
        Double-Your-Money-Back Man

        Baby be with me
        Everything's gonna be
                        alright
        Long as you
        be
          with
        us
        and if you stay
        everything be righteous
        from now on
        every word and every
                        deed
        if you
        be
        with
        us

        And when Jack came of age there was
a mortgage on
    the Diamond place and Jack went into town to clear it
and he was caught
                in
                the
            world's
        first ANNUAL
        JACK O. DIAMONDS RACE
                                and he
knew it . . .
            Time came they went and they got Jack,
brought him in on
    the end of a stick. They sent the mortgage in and they
had him.
    Jack was beginning to hear the
                        tick.

                        .

                tick.

                    .

                    tick.

_____
72

when he developed a sense of direction

    "Next time they
    get me I'm gonna ask
    but one thing:
        Please
            Reimburse
    the previous institution
      brought me thus far"
whereupon the judge said
      "You're worth twice
    as much as you were before"
and to Jack it sounded like a good thing

    ". . . worth twice
    as much as you were before"

And they brought the parade
          way
            Down
               Broadway
   (it was friendly as a railroad)
        until he
climbed from one
  thousand by twos to sixty four—
    Now what are you going to do
      with a sixty four thousand dollar
  man ?
    You're going to hand him the bottle and
  say
    *

      " Now you pour"
   You name your price now, Jack
   The world's yours for the taking
   Just look out for
       lying
         stealing
           and
breaking
   and don't forget—
     you're a friend
 now that you are travellin'

What happened to the mortgage?
Up before your eyes,
traded in a card game
(was the most important
card game of the year)
involved the Ace of Spades,
the King of Clubs, the Queen
of Hearts and
                    the
                        ten
        AND
            it
                involved
                            a
        Double-Your-Money-Back Man
    What did Jack do?
    He sent a letter to the Sheriff and he
signed it Marshall
    Dillon.   In the letter he said

            Dear Sheriff,
                Please send him on over. It comes
            to somethin' over a million dollars.

    And Jack, he disappeared on the Diamond City Stage
                and he has lived there
                to a ripe old age
                and when we saw him
                we heard him say
                    Now I raised
                    three sons to manhood
                    The four of us,
                    we did ride
                    into Nevada.
                    'I'm givin' you each
                    one silver dollar,
                    it may teach you a lesson.'
            And the oldest he won
            And the second he lost
            And the third, he went
            up to a stranger and said

'I'm a Double-Your-Money-Back Man'
and the stranger gave him a dollar and
Jack, he gave
the stranger back two! The stranger said
"I would give anything
to know what you do"
He said
"That will be two dollars"

And the stranger gave the two dollars to
Jack and the two
of them went up to a third stranger and said . . .
. . .

. . .
Well they were up to sixty four when I
stepped in and said
"Let's get outa here.
It's all in knowing
when to quit."

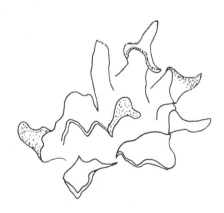

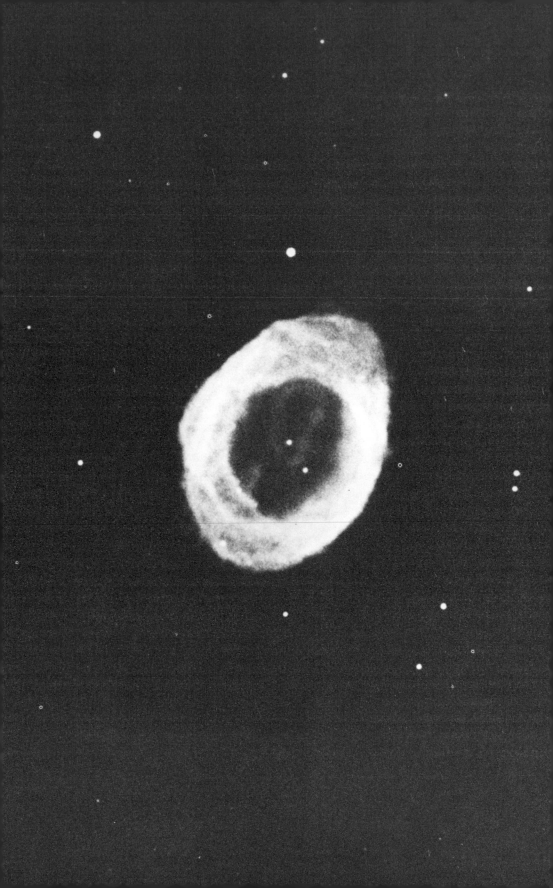

THE
FOURTH LAW

MONEY IS A NIGHTMARE: In
Jail, Robbery, Fears of Poverty

Those who went to the Demise Party of *The Whole Earth Catalog* in 1971 got an idea of what a downer money can be. (See article on the Demise Party at the end of the 5th Law.) But what happened at the party doesn't fully illustrate the horror of it. Hugh Hefner may be a good example, but not everybody would recognize that. A better example might be people in jail who are living a nightmare because of their involvement with money. About ninety percent of all crimes are committed because of money (I looked this up a few days ago), and about eighty percent of all people in jail are there because of money-related crimes. Eighty percent of all crimes consist of robbery, burglary, larceny, forgery and auto theft. A few other things which push the percentage even higher are murders, especially family murders, which have to do with money, and assault and battery crimes in which theft is a motive. Money is a very significant reason for people being in jail. Maybe one way of stating it is that their aspiration for money and their ability to accumulate it are radically different. People who commit a crime often reach a state where they want money so badly that they are willing to take a higher risk than most other people are. In my opinion, a person who gets caught stealing money from a bank or a grocery store is a person who has a fantasy about what money can do for him. I find it hard to understand how someone can hold up a bank or a grocery store simply because he is hungry. I myself and many of my friends have survived hunger for long periods of time without finding it necessary to harm or threaten other people. Many people in the world live at a subsistence level that is only a fraction of that which most Americans in jail have ever lived at. Again, it is hard to believe that what a con considers to be a "subsistence level" is worth stealing to maintain, or that his need to steal in order to maintain it is in any way related to reality. Money is clearly a nightmare for those who are in jail as a result of money-related problems.

Many marriages and divorces are obviously related to money and to what it does to people who try to work out some mutual arrangement for it. Most lawyers can testify to horror stories of what money can do to heirs and heiresses and of how they can destroy whole family structures in trying to get a piece of it for themselves.

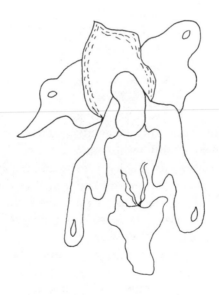

THE PAINTER

There was a painter, and he wanted very much to be rich and famous. But he had no oils.

In a window of a shop on a corner he saw the oils he needed. He broke the window, took his needs and wants, and ran.

After about a year he still was poor and wanting fame and, again, he found himself with no oils. He went to the shop on the corner and in the window:

RENT or LEASE
STORE
or
OFFICE SPACE

So he went to see a friend. His friend was a little poor and wanting fame too, but he had oils. He waited and waited while his friend painted and painted until friend fell asleep. Then he stole the oils.

After about a year the painter suddenly became popular, and after about another year he was rich and famous. Then he went to find his friend and he took many many oils with him.

Oh, friend said, thanks, but I don't paint anymore.

"If you pick up a starving dog and
make him prosperous, he will not bite
you. This is the principal difference
between a dog and a man."

Mark Twain, *Pudd'nhead Wilson's Calendar*

Salli and Barbara, my secretary, dislike my explanation
of the Fourth Law—that money is a nightmare—because I
describe prisoners as examples of this nightmare. Barbara
dislikes it because she spent many years in prison. Salli dislikes it because she feels there is an element of condescen-
sion in the phrase "Many of my friends have survived hunger for long periods of time without finding it necessary to
harm or threaten other people." And yet, in Barbara's case,
I think I couldn't find a more explicit example of how prisoners live out a money-related nightmare. Here is a woman
who was in jail several years, from age 16 to 24. She went to jail
because she was rebellious and defiant, but today, in her forties, she is one of the most conservative people I know—financially and politically. At some point she decided she was never
going back to jail, and from that day on she worked hard and
saved her money and obeyed almost every Ben Franklin dis-
cipline. Barbara reacts *very* strongly to people who are ex-cons
and brag about it, people who brag about how they cheat other
people through money deals. She has a very finely balanced,
continually-operating sense of people and their ethical behavior in terms of money. I didn't know Barbara as a young
woman, but her present behavior strikes me as a reaction to the
money-related behavior she encountered in jail.

Salli's point is a little harder for me to deal with, because
what she is saying is, Michael, don't you take into considera-
tion the fact that some of these cons have never realized that
their grasp of reality was going to end them up in jail—or

80

that their perceptions were wrong at all? In other words, they are trapped with a view of reality that has no built-in corrections. Their friends have the same views that they do and their parents have the same views, so they have no possible way to judge other reality perceptions.

My answer is reflected by the following chain of thought. All societies have deviant parts of their populations, and they are deviant for certain reasons. One major category of deviance in our society has to do with that part of the population which cannot deal with our cohesive tie, the unwritten laws, which have to do with money. Biological selection (survival of the fittest) operates in the same way. The money-deviance-jail process is the cultural equivalent of the biological selection process.

When I talk about a child that dies at two years old because of malfunctioning kidneys or an infant that dies three hours after birth because of heart failure, I don't expect people to regard this as a moral judgment. There's a survival-selection process operating biologically, and a certain percentage of infants who are born will die before they are two weeks old and another smaller percentage of them will die before they are three years old. It's neither a reflection on the parents nor a reflection on our culture that this happens. (It can be a measure of the development stage of the culture, and it's also a partial measure of what is happening in the evolutionary development of our species.)

The same thing applies to the people we put in a jail. This is part of the evolutionary development of the social fabric of the culture.

I am not expressing a moral judgment. I am making very clear something that many people aren't conscious of: among the people we punish, the people we have to take out of society, 80% or more are people who are unable to deal with money. There's no emphasis on that in criminology, and when the President of the United States (R. M. Nixon in 1973) talks about harsh penalties as an answer to rising crime rates, he doesn't mention peoples' inability to deal with money. When over-zealous liberals talk about the conditions that breed crime in the ghettos, they speak of pouring money in to give people nice houses, thinking that will solve the problems. Just from reading the first part of the First Law it should be clear that this is misleading. Most crime has something to do with the person's own conceptions about money, what he feels he's "entitled to" or "deserves" in contrast to what he's capable of getting. When this contrast is too great, when a person's desires and wishes are significantly different from his capabilities and skills, there's going to emerge a behavior pattern that will be punished by the society.

Let me give you the case of Dirk and Wolf, two people who made my life hell for a few months. Dirk and Wolf came to Glide with an extremely captivating proposal to create a school for ex-cons, making it possible for them to learn to survive on the outside. Both men were charming, verbal, black, and able to think very quickly. They were given a lot of staff help and $15,000 to get their program started. They worked closely with Cecil, a brilliant black minister on our staff who worked closely with the community. Dirk and Wolf came from ghetto areas, and Cecil didn't. He was willing to let them have almost anything they wanted if they believed they would be able to work more effectively in their own community. The whites on our staff, including me, recognized that we didn't know what poor blacks were about and let them go their way. The resulting policy was that Dirk and Wolf should be allowed almost free rein. When they wanted brand new leased cars, we all acquiesced to the logic that they needed the prestige such cars would bring in their community to be able to organize. When they needed expense accounts we operated on the assumption that we would have to have a "trust" situation in order for the program to work and that if we trusted them they would begin to deserve that trust.

What actually happened was that they would come up with some scam to rip off some money, and it would take me a week to see through it. In the meantime I was operating on a basis of trust. I would finally confront them with the evidence, and they would come up with some new scam. For example, after not receiving any expense receipts during the first week I told them that I needed receipts in order for them to get their expenses refunded. So they started turning in gas receipts. That was fine, until I began to realize that it was impossible for any car to put on as much mileage as was indicated by their gasoline bills and that they'd simply been stealing blank gasoline receipts and filling them in. The same applied to food and to other expenses. Week after week they had new scams.

After a while we found they were paying wages to assistants. That made sense to us until one of the assistants squealed that there was an extortion racket going on—the assistants were paid $150 for a week's work but had to kick back $75 to Dirk or Wolf.

In the end when we fired them Dirk came in and picked up Wolf's paycheck, and then Wolf came in the next week and said "Where's my paycheck?" We even proved that Dirk forged the signature.

This scam went on for a long time, and involved threats, guns and belligerence. Wolf threatened to shoot me. Next they stole the leased cars. They were knowledgeable enough to know that since we leased them it was not straight car theft; it was "conversion," which is not a felony but which kept the insurance companies from having to pay us off. Let's say it just went on and on.

Dirk and Wolf were well paid, but they doubled their salary through their fraud. They were such bright and charming people that they could have had a high salary in almost any conventional business. At each point, though, they always wanted money instantly, not realizing they would always have gotten more money if they had just been able to wait a little. It was more important to them to have an FM stereo radio in their car than to realize that in the process of coercing the FM stereo out of me and bugging (and threatening) me they would lose all prospects of keeping their job. The last I heard of them, a year later, Dirk had been shot in the leg by someone he had trouble with and Wolf was running an upholstery shop that seemed to be a cover-up for a burglary racket.

The main lesson that I would draw from these two men, both skilled, charming, capable people, is that they have such a completely distorted view of what they "need" that there is no way they can function in society. A minor adjustment in their sense of reality would have made them capable of functioning in a useful, viable way.

I later came to understand something about prison mentality from talking to Willie, who runs the Prisoners' Union. I told him the story of Dirk and Wolf. He said "Oh that's easy to understand, easy. Around my place we pay each of the ex-cons $10 a week, that's it, and we all live at that level. For Thanksgiving dinner I said, "All right you guys, I'm going to treat you to dinner. We'll go down to such and such a restaurant in the Mission district." (Which in San Francisco is one of the new immigrant districts.) A lot of the guys said "Man, we can't eat dinner there; we can't be seen there. We ain't going to Thanksgiving dinner in that place." I asked him why, and he said "That's what you've got to learn to understand. These guys are out on the streets. They almost know for sure that they're going back to the joint, and the prisoners are their peers, and when they get back to the joint they want to be able to say, *Man, I really lived well when I was out. I really had a great time. I lived high.*" And that's what you didn't understand about Dirk and Wolf. They knew that they were living in a fantasy world because their real world was back in the joint where everybody talks about the fantasy lives that they played out when they were outside".

Later on, when Wolf came to my office one day, I asked him to read what I had written about him. Then I taped his answer, with him making comments on the manuscript while he was reading it. (He was in my office to get me to have some chairs re-upholstered, so the conversations get mixed.)

WOLF (reading): No, I'm not signing nothing!
PHILLIPS: I don't want you to sign it, I just want you to tell your side of the story.
WOLF (reading again): Ooh, this is libel, slander, oooooh, detrimental of character. Mike, why you like that? (Pause. Laughs. He reads a part where it says he and Dirk could have gotten very good jobs if they had held on a while.)

Oooh, all we have to do is wait a little while—well no one told me that.

PHILLIPS: (Laughs.)

WOLF (reading on): This'll send me back to the penitentiary. (Laughs)

WOLF (finished): I'll tell you what, we goin' beef it up. I might go along with it if we get out on the boat (Mike's sailboat) and we add another chapter to it—add my side of the story.

PHILLIPS: *Tell* me your side of the story.

WOLF: What I had in mind when I created the ex-con school was something like there was over 1,200 people being released from penitentiaries. California has more institutions letting people out and they go in the least controllable situations, so I wanted a place for them, I wanted funds to build the City.

PHILLIPS: To build a City for ex-cons?

WOLF: The City.

PHILLIPS: Where is that idea now?

WOLF: I blew it. But it may not be too late; that's why I want to get on the boat and give you my version of the story. I don't mind what you said—you know, like, like not yet, 'long as you think I'm "Wolf," because I'm Eldridge Carver now, just straight, and don't put that stuff in the book. Why, what makes you think my shop's a cover-up for a burglary?

PHILLIPS: I think there's nothing you could do that's honest.

WOLF: No, my stuff's quality work, Mike, quality. In fact next week I'm goin' talk with a big furniture store to start with, I mean a couple big orders is what I'll get. This is what's been keepin' me from havin' to stay off the streets.

PHILLIPS: How can you change—how do you figure me to believe you changed?

WOLF: You come see my shop.

PHILLIPS: No, no, I believe there's a shop.

WOLF: I mean, you come see my work. Now Mike, about the chairs—here's the materials to choose. How many did you have planned, which chairs?

PHILLIPS: Two, there's two whole chairs which we're going to need.

85

WOLF: Let me look at the chairs, can I?

PHILLIPS: O.K., I'll let you look at them. Anyway, you haven't got any more kind of answers on the book? You don't want to tell me anything?

WOLF: When I get on the boat (laughs).

PHILLIPS: You ought to at least say, "Hey, we didn't steal a car "or something.

WOLF: But we didn't. I'll tell you why we held on to the car. You see, and then you can say "After having an extensive interview with Wolf," you see what I'm saying, then you build this shit up and I can ask for 15% and it's all legal and then they say "Well, the guy's not a crook; people *can* misjudge convicts."

PHILLIPS: (Whistles) Let me have that one again.

WOLF: I'm not going back in (the pen). I have my business to run, that's why I'm workin' up a sweat. I'm minding my own business but I gotta run it to you--the fact that I was in jail for a long time, that's what can really get you. I mean three years I thought about this shit, you know what I mean, so I wasn't going to go back.

PHILLIPS: How do you explain the fact that you got charm and grace . . .?

WOLF: charm and *ability*. . .

PHILLIPS: And you could get any job you want if you would just do it straight for three months?

WOLF: Mike, I got six years as a draftsman. I know how the pipe lines run on the streets; I did about a year and a half work on BART from 7th to 10th Street where they got the hidden cables. I know how to go through the roof tops of the buildings—I can do those things. I used to build like that but then, like, in my head, I said "O. K. if I could do it for say this big company, why can't I do it for myself?" So my grandfather got me involved in something when I was about eight years old, you know, handing down old furniture and stuff and I'd be running and guarding and watching him. After, they sent me to the joint where they put me, then I came out here. I was tired of fighting the police and all the bullshit and I figured I'd just open up a business.

PHILLIPS (Finding material he likes for re-upholstering):

How expensive is this?

WOLF: This here, this will run you $9.95. I could probably get it for you for $5.00.

PHILLIPS: What, $5.00?

WOLF: Yeah, you let me make a profit off the $9.95?

PHILLIPS: I'm tryin' to find out whether you're honest now. How can you ask me to—it doesn't matter.

WOLF: Look 'cause, the furniture—it doesn't matter. I'll tell you something: the furniture racket is the biggest racket in the world, man. You can take some old driftwood and make a couch, and charge you, man, fifteen hundred or something like this for somethin' that didn't cost you more than fifty bucks—add labor, you know.

PHILLIPS: (Laughs) That's true.

WOLF: I'm serious; then that's when I really found out I was honest.

PHILLIPS: (Laughs heartily)

WOLF: That—that's the truth.

PHILLIPS: So you felt 'cause everybody else is so crooked, you're honest.

WOLF: Yeah, it's real. Oh, and I might need a favor from you too. In order to talk with Mr.— (of a furniture store) I'm goin' need my license, you know.

PHILLIPS: What kind of license?

WOLF: Operating license. I have to have all of that Board of Equalization and it takes a hundred bucks, you know, so give me $50.00. How many chairs you have?

PHILLIPS: Two.

WOLF: Two. Well that's . . .

PHILLIPS: No advance! After all my experiences with you—

WOLF: Hey, Mike, next week I got some people who'er goin' buy me a suit and a tie.

PHILLIPS: I believe you, but with all my experience with you I'm not going to make an advance.

WOLF: Hey, I'm willing to take 25% interest, man.

PHILLIPS: I'm not going to get involved with you in any way. I'll give you the chairs.

WOLF: I knew, I knew you wouldn't.

PHILLIPS: I'll let you take them.

WOLF: O.K.

PHILLIPS: Actually, in the beginning of the ex-con school, I wasn't the one who was in favor of giving you any money—

WOLF: You know what it was—

PHILLIPS: Bob was the one.

WOLF: What happened was, and I'm goin' to be frank wit ya—drugs became involved, you see what I'm sayin', and instead of me making the stand I should have, I let it go on—it's just like Machiavelli says in *The Prince*, when you say you try to avoid something and it just gets worse, well that's what I experienced in this here situation.

Money is also a nightmare when looked at from the opposite perspective—from the point of view of people who have inherited a lot of money.

The Western dream is to have a lot of money, and then you can lead a life of leisure and happiness. Nothing in my experience could be further from the truth.

A friend of mine, Debbi, lives in Dallas, a very attractive young heiress who inherited a substantial amount of money from an oil fortune. She is an extremely sensitive woman, delicate, understanding, tender, and just miserable. As unhappy as she can be. She went to a fine school and she has a good education, but she can't even find a job that's meaningful. She lives in a nice apartment. She wants to associate with important people and she has enough money to do so, but she is hesitant about being friendly with people because she is afraid of being used by them.

Debbi doesn't have any clear idea of what to do with her life. She had all that money given to her at a point where she had never had a chance to find out what her life meant and what her reasons for existence were. Every day she goes out and looks for jobs and talks to people, and every night she goes home alone. Debbi never has to worry where her meals are coming from or where the rent's going to come from, but she must always be in constant terror that anybody who gets to know her will find out she has money and will use her. And that terror contributes only a small part to the lack in her existence of any sense of what she can do to become more of a person. There's always the feeling in her "Well, look, if I can't do it easily maybe I should just hire somebody else to do it for me." There are none of life's uncertainities, not much of give and take. "Why did fate choose me? Why do I have money when other people don't?" She moans. It's what Norman Mailer calls the Bryn Mawr syndrome. It's the Bryn Mawr graduate who commits suicide because the rest of the world is suffering.

Debbi inevitably has to ask herself the question "Why am I so well off? What have I done when there are all these other people I know, and respect, who have to struggle?" This guilt, this lack of understanding, this sense of responsibility for her money and not knowing how to use it to relieve other people's suffering and, most of all, her own, leads her to deep remorse. When she gives money away people become lecherous and latch on to her and won't let her go. They want more. She is merely reticent, but people treat her as if she were shy, and some are even unwilling to look at her as a person. She's in a rut, in a bind. If most people knew her well they would come to doubt that an inheritance is something beneficial.

Let me tell you about another well-to-do woman, Gina. Gina had received a substantial grant because of her involvement in the new schools movement, an area she had shown some interest in but in which she wasn't particularly active. Up to that point in her life she had been able to cope. She had a child, a husband, and played tennis. From the time she got the grant (which meant that she was expected to "do something," though nothing was specified), until the present she has been in a state of near desperation. She has been spending the money on therapy and on counselling of many types. Her nuclear family is beginning to disintegrate and she has had an emotional collapse on several occasions. Why? Because she was forced to ask herself, now that she had been given money with expectations attached "Who am I? What am I capable of doing? Why am I different in that I was given this grant and other people weren't?" These questions totally paralyzed her. She was never able to resolve them, and the stress has increased, although I am sure that in time they will be resolved. Gina's case is a beautiful example of the fact that getting money can be a nightmare.

Part of the reason why receiving money that is not a result of your own efforts is such a curse has to do with Laws Five and Six. That is because the donor, the person who gave it to you, has some implicit expectations of you, and it's impossible for you to live up to them, often because they are expectations that are not within your life experience. In the case of Debbi, the woman in Dallas, let's just presume that the grandfather who left her his money did so because he wanted to fulfill his desire to make his family like the Rothschilds—to have money and power for a long time—and because he wanted to justify his own accumulation of money. He needed to feel that his own life was justifiable, by the way he passed his money on. Now if he had asked his granddaughter point blank to live a life that he felt would have justified his accumulation of large sums of money or justified his desire to create a family like the Rothschilds, there would have been no way that Debbi could have accepted that responsibility. However, he didn't ask her point blank but instead tried to manipulate her by leaving his money to her instead of giving it to charity. Debbi exists without realizing that when she accepted her inheritance she accepted an implicit agreement with her deceased benefactor. Even if she could recognize the bind she is in she wouldn't be able to carry out her grandfather's wishes; if she did it wouldn't be her life but his fantasy of what her life should be.

This is not unrelated to the discussion under the First Law of what happens to some artists when they are too well rewarded for their work. Like the heir who can no longer look clearly at himself or herself, the successful young artist is stuck in a rut with his existing art form, and the rewards he gets for it keep him from being able to develop further.

There's another recurring nightmare that happens to millions of couples who work and save and scrape for their retirement. These people put aside their pleasures while young, amassing their money so that their retirement years can be comfortable. They sacrifice the joy of youth for an illusion of security. Many of these people come to realize too late that they have spent the bulk of their lives lusting for retirement. There must be considerable anguish in coming to this realization near the end of life. Think of their desperate attempts to have fun now that they have forgotten how. Is this not an example of money as a nightmare? (Erik Erikson claims that this crisis of old age is resolved by simple deciding that everything worked out O.K. Ha!)

A while back a woman who had grown up in a well-to-do suburban Philadelphia family came to my office. She had always been given anything she wanted and her every whim and desire had been satisfied. Why did she come to me? She wanted to start a camp where she and all her friends could hang out. She well knew she could raise the money, but what she was looking for was somebody who would actually do the work of starting and running the camp. I have seldom been so struck with a woman; she was a total sump. When we were together she drained every bit of energy that I could muster. In her life every whim was gratified, leaving her in a complete hole that drained the energy of everyone around her. In desperation, I think, she was trying to re-enact the one part of her life that had been fun—an early camping experience. The rest of her life had been stolen from her by readily-available money and the consequent lack of passions in her existence.

How does money become a nightmare for the ordinary working person? The treadmill is a common example. People work hard to provide themselves and their families with worldly goods, new and better toys, better appliances. It's the something we joke about so often—keeping up with the Joneses. Yet the process of working for more money so consumes our time and is considered so valid by our peers that we never stop to examine our values, our priorities. Even when people carry the Protestant work ethic to extremes we never question what they are doing. I'll elaborate a little; after all this *does* include most of us.

A man came into my office in desperate need of a loan. He was working fanatically on a business venture—one that was not a bad idea but which was obviously not immediately feasible; it would take from five to ten years to accomplish. He thought he had gotten promises from the Bank of America and American Express for help on his idea, but I knew from my experience with these companies that what they had really said was "If you get this, this, and this, then come back to see us and we'll take a more careful look." He had gotten dozens of corporations strung out with his idea and gotten that sort of nebulous promise. Each time a corporation said "Great" the prospect of imminent success got closer in his mind. He was living a fantasy. He was borrowing extensively and was enormously in debt. He had told only his wife about the financial strait that he was in; he had not told his children, nor did any of his friends and neighbors know to what extent his ambition had taken him. He scheduled meetings just before noon so he could be taken out to lunch and thus save money. He stayed up late at night so his children wouldn't see him starching and ironing his own shirts because he could no longer afford to send them to a laundry.

Since almost no answer I could give him would have been much less painful, I told him frankly that bankruptcy was a perfectly sound answer to his problems. I wanted him to realize that if he ever faced the fact that he *could* go through bankruptcy most of the people to whom he was in debt would probably accept him as a realistic person and allow him to work out his debt without actually having to go into bankruptcy. I felt that he would probably find that his children would support him completely and that they would be willing to give up an awful lot to help, as would his wife and his friends. He didn't have to drive a fancy car and look like a successful businessman in order to work on his idea. I felt he should look at all the things he valued and cherished and realize the pain he created for himself because he had placed money goals above family values. He had created a nightmare, and he was in incredible pain.

Money nightmares can arise out of the simplest relationships between people. Since I've been on the Board of POINT, I have had four or five bitter attacks directed at me, because I have access to money. One woman took me to lunch and proceeded to bawl me out because I hadn't given her money for her project, which she felt was obviously the most important thing in the world. She was furious that I was giving grants to other projects and not to hers. Now the fact that that hurt me in some way is my own fault. The reason I was hurt was because up to that point she had been a close friend, and now she was literally saying that my behavior in making grants to projects that appealed to me was causing her pain. I knew this was not true, but the lunch was agony.

At one point, Warehouse Project, a community warehouse group that had been operating for a year wanted me to give them money. I'd considered giving a grant, but I felt the idea had low priority and my intuition said no. One night I visited them, and when I sat down three people told me how terrible I was for not giving them any money. These were ordinary human beings; you'd probably love them. But because their project was so important to them and I was in a position of having money available as a foundation donor I was treated viciously. Their main argument was that if I was a friend why shouldn't I be willing to help them out with money? I tried to point out to them that the sad thing to me was that people failed to realize they saw me only as a source of money and not as a human being capable of giving them other help, of working with them in any other capacity except as a donor of money. I have a lot of skills for helping people get projects under way, and the thing that was the most painful in this case, and in several other cases, was the fact that some of my so-called friends saw me only as a source of money and not as a broader human being. I felt just the way my heiress friend feels.

How do you keep money from being a nightmare? How do you deal with money nightmares in the first place?

Probably my answer would be a dose of the first three Laws:

1) First, recognize that the values in your life have to be powerful, tangible values that exist independently of money.

2) Second, you must realize that there are underlying relationships between you and the world around you. These

93

should be reflected in your behavior in dealing with money—all the way from keeping books to being honest with yourself about your monetary perceptions.

3) Third, you should recognize, hopefully with a sense of humor, that money is a dream, that it's absolutely fantasy-like. When at any point you begin to substitute money as a goal, as a motivating factor, for the more important things in your life, you may end up in pain. And "nightmare," the Fourth Law, comes about as a consequence of violating the first three Laws.

Lolly

I am a twenty-nine year old woman with about $200,000 in personal assets, which yield an annual income of around $10,000. I also have about $5,000 in annual income from trusts I don't control. I have never been married. And I didn't earn my assets except by being born into the right circumstances.

This fact is difficult to say flat out. Few people know about it. I prefer it that way. Which is not to say that my money isn't riding around in front of me but instead that I want to control that particular bit of information.

I am afraid, I suppose, of being considered rich, a word which I do not use about myself even to myself. In some of the places I've been the fact that I have money would set me apart, would create envy and resentment and might well set me up for a hustle. In other places I might be thought of as pleasant enough but not worth even considering as a rich person. I have enough money to experience some of its disadvantages, but not enough to allow me to be particularly extravagant, at least not more than once. I like money: having it, making it, and sometimes spending it. But it does affect me. And just as I can't keep amounts completely straight I have trouble being entirely clear about its effect.

What I am clear about is:

1) I want to hang on to my money. I have been called tight-fisted. I want to make or have more of it, but not necessarily a lot more.

2) Not only do I want to hang on to money, I'm also quite attached to it. I have heard that we only have the use of money during our lifetimes but that it is not "ours". The stuff I have sure feels like mine; I don't feel particularly free about its coming and going.

3) Money does, however, buy me a kind of freedom. A freedom to thumb my nose at people who would try to pressure me economically if I became too threatening to them. And a freedom to find out what I want to do, because at

times I can do and have done absolutely nothing. Those freedoms can send me way up or down: they can make me exhilarated or heavy with what a Peanuts cartoon called "the burden of a great potential."

4) I do not want to expend a lot of energy on money.

5) I do not like to talk about my money unless I know someone fairly well. But then when I start I sometimes won't stop.

6) I have a rather strong conviction that I'm special, different, a cut above the other people—not that I like myself any better than the average mildly masochistic American likes himself. Although I'm ashamed of the times I have been snobbish, I am definitely a snob. The horror that I have when I see myself as being like everyone else has a lot to do, I suspect, with my money.

7) I do not like ostentation, although I can forgive it more easily in those who don't have money than in those who do.

I have wondered where I'd be without money. Actually, I have an idea. For the first five years after college I worked. At that point I had about $2,000 a year in "unearned" income, which I only used once. The nest egg was there, but I lived on what I earned. I let my jobs define me; I was ambitious in a career way, although I hated the word career. I always assumed that I would work after college at least until I got married, which I never did. Although I knew I could fall back on my parents if I really needed to, I assumed I wouldn't. My father says he values his children's independence. I was and still am proud of mine.

The direction I chose to go in led me to programs which aided the poor and the blacks. This may have been a sort of "noblesse oblige," although I hope not. It may have been a channel for me to express a personal anger in the milieu of the justifiable anger of the oppressed. It may have been wanting to save the world instead of myself, or, most likely, wanting to be useful and helpful. In spite of the bad name "doing good" has gotten, I, like a lot of other people, want to do good—to do something that will make a difference. Whatever the motivation, the jobs gave me an education about some facts of life that money had sheltered me from. I do not, for example, romanticize or even like poverty, for myself or anyone else. People who have money often think that it is the fault of poor people that they are poor. I would say it is probably more our fault: "our" in this instance meaning the haves. I also found that people *are* people; money isn't everything, but that's easier to say when you have it.

I have felt a conflict when working with or talking to people who have much less money than I do, a reaction felt by any reasonably sensitive American travelling in a very poor area. I am aware of the huge difference between the way I spend a dollar and the way some others have to scrape to earn it. I am also, of course, aware of the resentment I create. In fact, I can understand, although I don't condone, the isolation of richer people from much poorer people.

But the discomfort does not come merely from a fear of being disliked, nor just from a feeling of guilt about having more money, but from an unwillingness to part with much of it. The problem, obviously, would not exist if I were to give all my money away. I don't, because I know it wouldn't make any difference. I also don't because I don't want to.

What I have concluded about the guilt/responsibility question is that my money is one fact of my existence. I had nothing to do with its being given to me. Nothing. Nor did I have anything to do with how the money came into being. But every time the abuse of a river, a tree, a customer, or an employee puts money in my pocket, I too am a culprit. The people who make the decisions of whether or not to pollute, cheat and discriminate say they do so in my name. I have tried to research some of the "social costs" of the money sources and present the information to other members of my family who might be able to do something. I am still continuing this effort, although I'm not satisfied with the results.

My sense of family, which is strong, has to do with relatives whom I know or have known. Although there are lots of relatives I don't particularly like, both sides of my family are quite family minded. Because enough relatives have had

97

genealogical streaks, I can trace my family back pretty far. But I don't have any sense of pedigree, for a good reason; I come from a typically American mishmash. None the less, in societal terms, I am somewhat statusy, although the status of waspy types has slipped in recent years.

My friends don't fit any particular pattern, but some of the men I've been with, especially in the last few years, have been less "statusy": Jews and blacks. I am not sure how to evaluate that—whether money has anything to do with it or if it's a function of the things I'm interested in. I do feel a little uncomfortable writing about status, me, and men; probably I see some sort of societally determined difference between me and them, and I probably have some residual prejudices. By other criteria, the men I have known have been as smart, wise, or sophisticated as I am—or more so. In any case, I think I've spent time with some pretty good people. Actually, I have a problem making any unqualified generalizations about the men I've been with, although I put a lot of energy into my relationships with men, usually with one man but never with him exclusively. And about 75% of the time it's the man who ends the relationship, status or no status.

One example of my money muddying things up with men is my fear that men might want me for my money. I've heard enough stories about hunting for a rich wife to make me wary. Actually, it's a question of degree; I don't have enough money to make it worth someone's while if he doesn't like me, and I've been dumped enough times to know that the money doesn't make that much difference. But I never know how much difference it does make. When the thought does enter my head it's an ugly one. It makes me suspicious and tight. It is, after all, a bummer to think that someone, especially a man, wants to be with me, to whatever degree, not because of me but because of my money. On the other hand, I, too, would just as soon spend my time with someone who has lots of money.

The reactions of men to my having money have varied from "I'd like to have it" to "Sure, it's attractive" to "I don't give a shit" to "I don't particularly envy you" to "It's an unattractive aspect of you" to anger at my prejudices.

I have also been told that I have ways of letting people know my situation. I've even caught myself at it.

I feel bad sometimes when people I know have money problems, especially the insoluble kind. I can see how the need for money can dull or destroy. A need for money which I would call excessive is making one man I know selfish, manipulative, and limited.

My current "honey" and I had a big discussion recently about my money and his feelings about it. We've had several other discussions: my feelings about my money, his feelings about money. He accuses me of class snobbism (some of which I admit to); I accuse him of class snobbism (some of which he admits to). This particular discussion came up because of a family discussion about how much money there was and what might happen to it. Although I generally have a hard time not blabbing about what's on my mind at any given moment, I was reluctant to get into it. I was afraid he'd like me less if he knew there might be less money. He had implied it before, and I suspected that he was interested in my money. When he finally got me to admit that I was asking if he was after my money, he answered yes. He said that to him my money was one of the attractive things about me. Yes, he wouldn't mind spending or having some of it. I asked him if my money made him act any differently toward me than he would otherwise. He said no. If money does stop him from being hostile, annoying or cold at times, it's not noticeable, He has said that I don't have enough money (but until he reads this, he doesn't know exactly how much there is) and that money by itself is not enough to interest him in anybody. On the other hand I can't help being suspicious—especially because his close friends tend to be rich. One new wrinkle since our discussion: when it seems he's being gratuitously unpleasant I wonder if it's because I told him he would never have any control over my money.

I should say about this particular friend that I think he is right: on balance money isn't that important a factor between us. It's there, but lots of other things outrank it.

A more recent postcript: He decided that he didn't want to marry me after all. The irony is that now I'm a little less suspicious of him.

Some thoughts I couldn't fit in anywhere else:

My money is like a big pillow or a soft blanket to fall back on or to wrap up in when I'm feeling low. Periodically, I get into moods during which I make desperate attempts to reach out and/or pull into myself. When one of these gets bad and my fantasies get more and more catatonic, I feel that I could just stay right here in my house forever. The truth is: I could. Now I have a job, so the current likelihood is that I wouldn't hole up in the house, but for several years I had absolutely no responsibilities. I am still too close to the years when I didn't have a full time job to be able to analyze, catalogue, and file them away. I do know that I was lonely then and am still lonely now, and continually plagued by the questions about the purpose of my existence. I realize that money does not have a monopoly on or even cause these questions. My money may have exacerbated such problems, because I do not *have* to go out. I can afford to isolate myself.

The distribution of wealth in this country is such that many people just don't have enough. Because of this people who have money are hated for having it, especially if we don't give it away, or are hassled if we do give it away. Part of the job I now have involves fund raising. Perhaps another irony. I hear people say things like "I don't give a shit about her; I just want her money," and I hear of resentment against "coupon clippers." I cringe somewhere inside.

Someone suggested that my money was destructive because I was rewarded for the wrong thing. I don't think it's so much a question of the wrong thing; I think everyone should be rewarded for being. But I have not earned my money, and to most Americans unearned goodies are akin to sin.

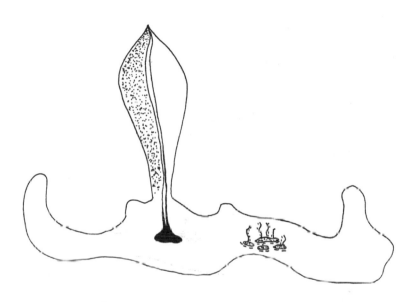

HOW THE SEVEN LAWS
DISCOVERED MONEY

Life is a struggle for evil
And for the righteous too
It's a struggle to do what's right
That's how it came to be

In the beginning, we were drinking a lot of beer—too much beer. Who was it cured us of drinking too much beer? It was the Wino, that's who, and we don't even know his name. For historical purposes, we don't even know his name, unless it is Given.

We were badly bloated, floating high in the pizza pie sky, crying out who will cure us of drinking too much beer? When down below he tugged at the kite string, he said

For thirty six cents I will
Yes I will.

And that ain't all, cause he came back with a bottle in a paper sack and showed us how to drink wine. We will tell you all we can of how it is done, but we do not recommend it—to anyone.

THE COLLECTION

There is a ritual around money. First thing a definite amount is set, generally known to all the participants, although we were unable to determine exactly who or how set the precise number, although we did establish the fact, evidently there are only a few numbers in common use—during the time interval in which our study was conducted these were 36, 54, and 69. We were told by several participants that 36 was for a short dog, 54 was for a large, and 69 was for "somethin' else."

THE RUN

The Collection involves not only the participants but many onlookers, bystanders and generally anyone in sight. As a rule, any who join in the Collection are invited to participate in the Ritual of drinking. However, only a trusted one or few (in some cases all) are chosen to make the Run. Upon completion of the Collection, the participants gathered in a circle, standing, and ascertaining that the correct Number has been collected. It is then that one or more of the participants are chosen to make the Run. The Run is made to the Store.

FIRST EXPERIENCE

Our first experience was with both a short dog and a large, in fact several. We ourselves made runs that first day. By the time the Store closed, we were unable to walk. We stretched out on the grass, and the street, the buildings, the lights, everything felt or looked fluid and flowering. The other participants stood in a circle, passing the last of a bottle and singing a chant, one of their numerous sacred songs, the words of which went something like

"Mama, Mama

And Your Mamoo too"

SECOND DAY

We woke with the sunrise. The light appeared to us somehow new and unbearably intense. We went home and slept. Later waking, we returned to find the Wino and other participants already into the Collection. He greeted us warmly, motioned us to approach closer to him, glanced sly right and sly left, then asked how much money we had. We explained that we had no money (which was not true) and that we did not wish to participate in the Ritual but only to observe as objectively as possible. He nodded and said "It's alright. You're with me."

EVASION

We brought out our notebooks and endeavored beginning our observations with the query
1) What is your name? However he evaded the question. Suppose we are asked by other participants, we asked him. Suppose they asked us:
1a) Who are you with? His reply was both evasive and emphatic. YOU are with me, he said. We decided not to pursue this line of inquiry any further at that time. It was Monday, five forty-five. One of the participants approached us, drew us to one side and immediately gave us his name. We shall call him Informant to protect our sources. However, that is not the name he gave us.

INFORMANT'S STORY

I'll tell you all you want to know about him. The Wino. You call him the Wino, all right, he probably has a thousand names, I see you coming, I understand why you are coming and you'll never get it, not from the Wino. Who's got it? Not me. One time pretty little girl here was saying her baby was in jail going to die and she wants and he needs help. You know what he said? He said,

---

103

I DEFINITELY PROMISE
you I will take care of it, as soon as you
give me 36 cents for a bottle to clarify
my brains."
That's what he said.

MORE LIES AND A TABOO

Cause he just wanted a case like hers as far from him as possible, I'm telling you like it is, but she DID give him, in fact about 75 cents, and he took it.

Informant grew nervous, then still, then started to sidle off, staring at our note-taking. We asked Informant if we were violating a taboo by taking notes, he insisted there was no taboo, that he had to return his energies to the Collection and could no longer stand around and talk to us.

Is that the whole story—about the Woman and the 75 cents?

No. She said Goodby Forever to that 75 cents, but he did get the Baby out of jail.

Yeah, how?

SCIENTIFIC METHOD

Informant insisted his energies were needed for the Collection, we could not keep him. Evidently our method was faulty. If we stayed out of it we might well mess up our relations with our one informant at that time, while if we jumped in again like we did the day before, we could taint our objectivity, due to the influence on the brains of the Ritual. We therefore decided to adopt the middle course and informed Informant of our decision, that we would contribute to the Collection but would remain as observers only, and we inquired whether he could not continue his story, along with the necessity of taking notes.

THE WHOLE STORY

On the way to the Store, for sure, and if not we'll kill it when we get back, Informant said.

However, despite promises and numerous queries, negotiations and promises on our part, it was only very late, after the Store had closed and after we ourselves—hoping thereby to elicit information from Informant —had joined in the Ritual that we uncovered as much of the story as ever was ours to learn.

The Wino and the Woman solicited friends young and old to appear in Court, some children supposed of the Baby, and also one woman conferred privately in chambers with the Judge on behalf of her brother (the Baby) and the Wino stood in Court and said he was Defendant's father and offered his own body as bail. These measures, however, proved only partially effective, there remained a reduced rock bottom sale price to pay in hard cash. The Judge was very cold.

Plans were considered either to entertain the Judge's daughter in hopes she could influence her father, or possibly to seek either a loan or a rebate (this point was not clear in Informant's own mind) from the Store. Yeah?

He paid it.

Who?

The Wino. He paid it. Paid the bail.

Where did he get it?

Don't ask me. If you don't know, O.K., just don't tell anybody I told you.

In the morning there was no sun to wake us up. All appeared fluid as before, ourselves too seemed part of the flow, but we sensed the sky beyond the clouds was different—there was above and there was below, otherwise we could not explain the rain. At home we remarked how we were beginning to look like participants in the Ritual and wondered if in time we might begin to understand their thoughts processed.

COOKING

I'm going, said the Wino, after whatever for a stew.

We went with him and took all our questions. First, was it true?

Then, where did it come from?

Why are we thirsty?

Does it mean that everything is a flow?

We explained that we must have answers.

You might make it yet, he said. But he did not respond to our questions at that time. We followed, gathering the makings of a stew. Some from gardens, some from stores, some from garbage cans. We returned and found a fire already going, water boiling. The Wino did the cooking and evaded all our questions, all he would say was "Please don't throw away the key."

THE GIFT

He made a very large stew in an old tub and several small mud pies in rusty tin cans and we ate from tin cans and old jars. Some have that gift.

They do.

They do.

I've seen them come and seek out one particular man. I mean come looking for him with a five or a ten in hand.

There's some if they fell out of a airplance and landed in the desert they'd find it, they'd make it.

Pick up old rocks an' walk into town an' set up a stand an' sell 'em.
I'm not gonna tell ya Jesus walked on these very stones. . . .

Because if I do, there are forces in this city that will arrest me and throw me into jail. . . .

Forces that resist the teaching. . . .

I'm not gonna tell you these stones slept with under the pillow in three weeks cure arthritis and rheumatism, and held in the hand and over the heart. . . .

In and out of recorded case histories cures and raises the dead, to walk over the foreheads and the blind to see. . . .

And in your purse, pocket, yes and bank safe deposit box generate silver and even gold coins fully engraved. . . .

For was there not a rock in Daniel's slingshot?

The Devil raises doubts. Too late! Once doubt and you're a child of God. Twice born into a new life. Three doubts and you're out.

The stew is gone! Where to? The cake is still here. Did anyone choose the cake over the stew? And why not?

From the earth all good with the requirements sky above and water below, moisture and thirst and thirst and drink. Don't eat of the earth as it is! Got to be cooked.

Amen.

The sun lit up the sky and it was none of it still, below lots of movement too, everywhere below, but the mudpie held steady, we took it home, it was real and solid under foot. It was getting up and walking and carrying something that did it.

WINO MISSING

Evening and the Wino was nowhere to be found. We could not inquire after him because we did not know his name. We observed Collection, Run and Ritual without him. Just after the Store closed he came looking for us.

"C'mon it's a party."

GLASSES

The Wino led us to a darkened house, and opened the door to peek in. He motioned us to follow. It was stone dark inside and we heard someone, a woman, walking in the room.

She said, You're back, wait a minute I'll light some candles.

We saw then the Woman sitting on a couch. Several big old cozy chairs and we saw that there was still a large jug of wine left untouched. It was a new Ritual for us. The Midnight Hours. We drank from glasses.

I want to thank you. Whatever the circumstances.

We could not speak, could not move, it was more than we had ever drunk before, it seemed we were drowning in a moonless night sea, nothing but to focus all will and thought upon the candle, force awake, sleep and wake, wake and sleep.

I see him in the candle, in the flame, running. I know it's going to be all right. That night I woke up, just when it happened. I knew it was happening when it happened. They say the Stars. Signs. Only thing you got to watch is follow the signs meant for you, if need be for you alone. It won't be easy. It will be true. For you it will be true.

SHOWDOWN

A bird sounded outside the house. Dawn, not yet sunrise, the moon hung up on the other side of the sky, waiting one eye open.

We left after sunrise, went home and slept. When we woke we took all our money and went to find the Wino, we explained the situation, except our money we kept secret, and again asked for his name and for instructions.Who am I?

What is my name?

My name is Given.

Look at this my hand, five you see.

The crossroads. This way because it is

what it is. But you still come and question it.

INSTRUCTIONS

First, give me all your money, whatever you have, tomorrow you can give it away, today you are to observe objectively how others give you money. Tomorrow you can divide it evenly, whatever is fair.

Remember, the fish need water.

Baby needs love.

The Creator needs time.

And if you want to be winos you need only one thing and that is wine.

No one has it all.

It is all ways even and it must always balance.

SHOES

We went on our way and the first body we stopped said:

I used to be in your shoes. Until the fish came after me. Everything was moving and fluid all the time. Then the ocean gave birth to all kinds. At first I thought they were after me. Then I discovered they don't care one way or another. Sometimes the fish would destroy a man and swim away, and fellow man, he too did not care one way or the other. That is how I found out. But I was nervous about it, terribly nervous, until at last I attacked one of them with a knife.

It was impossible to kill the fish, no matter how I slashed and jabbed out of my mind with blood, but I held on and it carried me up and up and up to where a huge bird was reeling in a line. The bird looked at me and said:"I'm going to give you the gift of life,"and threw me back in.

COINS

The body gave us some coins anyway. The next body also gave us coins. Then the body said:

I used to be in your shoes until I noticed, look very very carefully . . .do you see them?

The body showed us filaments on the coins, tails fine spun like spider webs.

It's hard to brush them off, to keep them off your skin and hair. In case I tripped over them and nearly choked to death.

The third body was barefoot and also gave us coins anyway. We had enough then for a bottle all our own. We made the Run and celebrated the Ritual. The morning was old and tired. We slept.

It is the same sun every day.

ENDANGERED SPECIES

Honesty is an endangered species, he said, and shook his head. Just now, not more than an hour ago, I divided the last time. I kept this for myself. . . .

(He showed us a few coins in his hand.)

. . . .one half. I kept one half each time I kept one half. We can still divide this ex ways, it's enough for a bottle for every one of us.

That was Given's story, so we decided his full name must be Given Away.

Nobody stayed around after copping a share, we have this all to ourselves.

Given Away, give us the whole of what you have left. We'll buy one big jug.

FRIEND OF KINGS

Given Away was in tears, he would not touch the wine we brought. All my life, he said, I have wanted to be a wino, a simple, dignified, aloof and independent wino. Even when I was a kid, I remember a story they told. Beholden to no man. Slave to none. When a disciple asked what is religion? he was told

like this—

A King went to a Wino friend of his and said
Here's a twenty—go buy us something to drink
You know as well as I do
The religion you live
That's the only religion you have
Every day full time
livin'
And the King gave the Wino his kingdom, but the Wino refused, saying he had no use for it, and he begged the King, Please, he said, say no more.

I command you, said the King, to take my kingdom.

The Wino said, I have no need to command. I know how to tie a knot, why should I show you how to do it?

I know how to cook.

I am beautiful and everything I have is beautiful
and
I do

what I want.

The King went away happy, knowing that he had a friend.

THAT'S NOT ALL

The kingdom prospered. A Prince was born. After fifteen years the Prince and his father, the King, dropped by the Wino's. The Prince stayed to drink wine. He stayed until the women spotted him and stole him away from the winos drinking wine.

Thereafter the Wino died. The King and the Prince came separately and met at the funeral. The Prince held in his hand a bottle of wine. The King went to his son, took the bottle and drank from it.

The rain falls, said the King, on me same as on you.

UNTOUCHED

Given Away went away, the bottle untouched. By morning we were thinking only of beer and we had not touched the wine. We slept and then we woke and went looking for Given Away to give him the jug of wine. We found him sleeping in the weeds behind a fence, painted on it the words

"Wino Power"

so we woke him and we said we would forgive him everything and we would give him the bottle if he would only explain the Seven Laws.

He could scarce open his eyes but he moistened his lips and managed to speak. Here is what he said:

The spirit of God moved upon the face of the waters.

And God said, let there be light, and the evening and the morning were the first day.

And God made the Firmament and the waters under from the waters above, the second day.

And He gathered together the dry land, grass and herbs and trees, the third.

The fourth He made the stars, the Sun and the Moon.

And God said, Let the waters bring forth the moving creatures, the fifth day.

And God made the beasts and every creeping thing, and He said, Let us make man in our own image, after our likeness, and He gave man dominion, the sixth day.

And on the seventh, He rested.

What do you think?

Give him the wine. Wine to the wino, milk to babies, junk to the junkies, tea to the tea drinkers, beer for the people, acid for acid heads, food for the hungry, faith for the faithful.

To each his own, and may we live in peace.

THE
FIFTH LAW

You can never really give money away.

COMMENTARY ON THE FIFTH LAW

I guess this law sounds bizarre on the face of it. Maybe I didn't realize how other people would interpret it when I wrote it. Salli reacted by saying that she thought it was because there's so much of it around. That's not really my view. I prefer to see money as a flow that can be seen in static or dynamic terms. In dynamic terms, money describes a relationship: borrower/lender, or seller/buyer, or parent/child. Looked at over a period of time, money flows in certain channels, like electricity though wires. The wires define the relationship, and the flow is the significant thing to look at. The Fifth Law comes from looking at money in this dynamic sense. We are used to seeing it in static terms, where we normally expect to see a two-directional flow associated with money. For example, I give the man behind the counter $18 and he rents me a Cessna 172 airplane to fly for an hour. We *expect* the two-directional flow, the exchange. Then we see someone who gives a friend $25.00 and says "keep it." We call that a "gift" because it is a one-directional flow, or at least it seems to be, in the context of a short period of time. The Fifth Law of Money suggests that by looking at the gift in a larger or longer term of perspective we will see that it is part of a two-way flow.

Dick Raymond likes the term "alliance" to describe the giving relationship. I think a lot of people can identify with that term. I feel more comfortable with the words "loan" or "investment" to describe the giving relationship. From a casual perspective, the lender gives the money and the borrower just signs a piece of paper. In a real-life giving situation, the piece of paper (loan note) and its contents are implicit in the situation but are not customarily talked about in our culture.

Many of these concepts have come out of my experiences in foundation work over two years, during which time I've given away over a hundred thousand dollars. Just saying that appalls me, because I can't even remember where most of the money went without systematically searching my mind or records. That sum of money sounds startling to me; I had probably never given away more than $5,000 to charity in my whole sweet life. In the case of the hundred thousand, I spent an inordinate number of hours thinking about the problem of giving and being very emotionally involved in the process. When I think of my good grants and bad grants, the bad ones that come to mind relate to situations where I gave money to someone or some project which appealed to me on an intellectual level but was not emotionally satisfying—something for which I didn't feel any passion and in which I was not involved. Conceptually, these were giving situations where the flow was one way, the loan was not repayed. Repayment, of course, was to be in emotional satisfaction.

One such grant was to a woman who headed her own organization. She made a spectacular initial impression on me because of her forthrightness and her outspokenness on corporate social responsibility. When I learned that she needed money for air fare to enable her to attend and speak out at a corporation's annual meeting, I provided the money. As it turned out, (1) I was not around to attend the meeting, and (2) she sent someone in her place. The outcome of the meeting was merely a little PR in the newspaper. Although I'm sure that dollar for dollar it was as useful to society as some comparable projects, I nevertheless felt pretty bad about the grant.

Later on, the more I got to know her, the more I found her to be a physically cold woman whom I could not feel very close to. As a consequence, I resolved that I wasn't going to give money to anybody whom I didn't feel emotionally strong and warm about, and that I wasn't going to give money when I couldn't be involved in the project.

The Board of POINT made several other bad grants from our point of view. One was to an individual who received a grant to work on feminists' issues and then never did a thing. Both the Board and she had far greater expectations of her abilities than it was possible for her to meet--which brought her close to a nervous breakdown. In a similar situation, another woman found the sensible solution and gave her grant back.

One of the interesting lessons Stewart Brand (who is also a POINT Board member) learned is that you don't give money to an idea. One of his worst grants was when he picked an idea rather than the person who was to carry out the idea. The idea was that a poor, fairly effective man could be made very effective by giving money to help him. He gave a $15,000 grant to a man who usually lived on $5,000 a year. The grant was blown in six months, and nothing happened; the guy just went back to looking for a job. In this case nothing happened The money changed hands—it was all seen as a one-way transaction by Stewart and his grantee. Stewart ended up with the pain of having made a poor grant.

Some of my very best grants have been made using Dick Raymond's concept of "alliance." One grant was to Alice Tepper Marlin, of the Council on Economic Priorities. Because of Alice's qualities and a close working relationship with her a number of good projects came out of our association. The grant to a strong individual *plus* the relationship was effective, powerful, and rewarding to all of us. Even after the end of the grant year Alice still hadn't used the full amount of her grant.

I don't wish to give the impression that POINT grants are calculated like loan agreements. As we've gone along, I've learned the emotional components of the giving business and have tried to keep the consequences out in the open. This openness is different from the policy of the traditional foundation, where there is often a secret string attached to grants. Without being open about it the traditional foundation has something specific that it wants done, and when it makes a grant, unless progress is made toward its unstated goals, the grant recipient is slowly tortured. What happens is that the grantee's ability to get more funds depends on how closely his project conforms to the Foundation's hidden agenda. Grants are usually renewable annually, and only in rare instances are they given for periods in excess of a year. The whole grant renewal concept is very much like the way a bank makes loans. Most bank commercial loans are only for 90 days. Banks always want the option of getting their money back if they are not satisfied with the way in which the borrower is operating. Doesn't granting sound like lending?

It has also been my experience in foundation work that the traditional foundation operates on the same basis that I do in terms of emotional components, without being open about it. Virtually all their grants go to people whom they already know and like—even when the actual grant is made in the name of an institution. I'd say POINT's most successful approach to money giving has been the open recognition that we are creating alliances with *people*. Out of our alliances we have developed some mutual goals without setting arbitrary criteria and objectives. We find our growth is therefore spontaneous—*not* as a result of money but as a result of our associations.

Ted McIlvenna and Lew Durham, two brilliant men who had a great deal of responsibility for establishing Glide Foundation in San Francisco, have long been aware that their most successful grants have to been individuals or to small groups of closely-knit associates.

One of their guiding concepts in the creation of Glide was that one of the most effective operatives in a society is not a person acting on his own, but one who has the continued support and interaction with colleagues. This collective approach parallels the concept of an alliance; money is not given away—an alliance is created.

Being put on the Board of POINT was a gift to me. I have viewed it as a two-way flow; my acceptance of the "responsibility" is my repayment. I have always kept in mind that the money came from *The Last Whole Earth Catalog* and that in some distinct sense its use is related to its origin. The origins of the money and the experiences with it have heavily influenced many Board members, particularly me.

The fund of one hundred sixty thousand dollars for completely discretionary personal grants, available to each board member, has caused me to re-evaluate and restructure my life. For the last two years I have been conscious of what my energy and money are supporting. I've had to decide what I consider to be most important—what my passions are, why I am alive and what I am going to do with the rest of my life. The questions could have been posed in an abstract way before I started, but the actual acceptance of responsibility for having the money forced me to answer the question and struggle with the outcome.

I accepted a responsibility when I accepted the money. I now am discovering what are the most effective things I can be doing to influence the world around me (or to influence *me*, which is another way of looking at it). In the process, I have had to modify my perceptions to the point where I can say I am satisfied with the validity of my image of the world. I have come to know that my image is stable enough and that it is clear enough to me, so that I can draw some conclusions about how my behavior will affect my surroundings.

I put part of this in writing, in the form of a memo to all POINT Board members submitted as part of the POINT records. The rest was in the form of changes in my life.

The not so obvious part of the struggle dealt with overcoming roadblocks: two were mentioned in the Third Law—the sign written in the desert with a tractor and the sex furniture that I paid $300 to have built. Doing this overcame my mental roadblocks, sort of opened the closed loops in my mind that had focused my energy on minor fantasy-like things in such a way that I couldn't get on to the major things.

117

I have to admit that the availability of money simply forced the issues, forced me to deal with the fact that I had to take on the small projects that I had emotionally committed myself to, as well as the large ones.

In daily life, it's not that different. There are a lot of things I have to do during the week, some pleasant, some unpleasant, some large, some small. Often the small, unpleasant ones are so obvious they keep me from doing the rest. Then I get a feeling of guilt from not doing the rest and I become depressed. I have slowly learned, after all these years of having to deal with this problem, that I have to change my behavior to the extent that I complete the unpleasant, small tasks with a determination that allows me to go on then to the other jobs. Otherwise, nothing will happen.

An analogy that Salli just came up with is perfect —if you don't do the dishes after each meal you finally end up having to do a huge pile of dishes that have stacked up.

Before ending this chapter on giving it might be interesting to mention that I got to thinking about "allowances" for children while writing this. When I was doing research in the Library of Congress I looked for money-and-children books and books on the subject of allowances. There was only one writer who had touched on the subject, and she had narrow perspectives with a great deal of vintage-1940 psychological advice. And yet allowances are damned important. They are given with the intention of shaping a child's personality, and they carry with them very strong implicit messages and expectations.

Just checking around my own neighborhood and asking the friends of my three children about their allowances I found a wide range of patterns. One family doesn't give allowances, but gives the kids large sums of money on birthdays and holidays. Another family gives the children large allowances, but also a list of "approved" items it can be spent on. Still another family ties the allowances to specific chores around the house; the more chores the more money. Some allowances are given just because the child exists; some are given out of guilt; some to teach money handling;

some to encourage responsibility for money; and some just to have another last-resort punishment, "I'll cut off your allowance." But, interestingly, I don't find much self-examination on our part as to what this parent-child-money relationship is.

Giving? The Fifth Law probably should be applied in our own homes first.

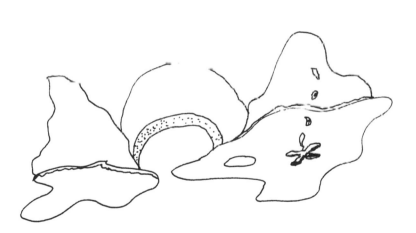

FOUNDATIONS GONE WILD

An example of foundations gone wild occurred recently. I funded Margo St. James to organize a prostitutes' collective to protect street prostitutes from the inhuman daily abuse they get from the police, the courts, and hypocrites. I advised her to let a few local foundations know what she was up to so they would be aware of her project if in the future she should need to go to them for funds. I read the letter she sent to them; no request, just a friendly letter saying what she was doing. One liberal foundation, Pacific Change, invited her over for lunch and grilled her cruelly and mercilessly the same way they do groups they regularly screen. They berated her for not being serious, not being a member of a minority and not being poor enough. Fortunately, she told them to go to hell and left. Another foundation simply sent her a letter of rejection, although she hadn't applied for money. These institutions are examples of how most foundations are so structured that they become numb in the process of dealing with the pain people feel in the donor/grantee relationship.

THE LAST TWELVE HOURS OF THE WHOLE EARTH

By Thomas Albright and Charles Perry

The Demise of the Whole Earth was a wake, and like any good wake it lasted until early morning, what with 1500 people haggling over the deceased's estate.

The estate—a wad of 200 $100 bills—was a surprise "educational event" sprung by Whole Earth Catalog founder Stewart Brand on the former Whole Earth employees, contributors and reviewers who had come to celebrate the publication of The Last Whole Earth Catalog. By the time of the party, June 12th, they had probably all digested an earlier educational event, Brand's decision a year and a half ago to stop publishing his successful Catalog this summer.

The $20,000, however, proved too much to deal with in a single night, and by 8 AM the 1500 guests dwindled to 20. In the end the 20 delegated one of their number to hold the money, which itself had dwindled to $14,905, until they could reconvene to decide what to do with it. He stuffed the money into his jeans and drove off into the sunrise.

In contrast to the San Francisco Trips Festival, which Brand co-authored with Ken Kesey five years ago to usher in a new era of weird drugs, hard rock and blinding, stroboscopic light, the Demise party belonged to another age—a future age which often harks back to a past one.

The 1500 invited "catalog makers" who filled the cavernous interior of the San Francisco Palace of Arts and Sciences, were mostly a quiet, sober, even saturnine crowd, like a group of mid-western dirt-farmers who had come to town on Saturday night to visit a country fair. They were a far-flung group of dirt-farmers, of course—from Seattle and Portland, the up-country wilds of British Columbia and the Southwest Desert. Here and there, one saw people shouldering sleeping bags or bedrolls, carrying hitchhike signs: "San Francisco" on one side, "Berkeley" or "Los Angeles" on the reverse.

A volley-ball game began early at one end of the blimp-hangar-like hall and continued almost without stop until late the next morning. There were intermittent bouts of boffing—jousting with styrofoam swords, hectic but harmless. In one corner, servers passed out fresh oranges, watermelon slices, apple cider and home-baked bread, and the refreshments were supplemented by bring-your-own gallon jugs of red wine.

A pair of display tables bore the tome-size Last Whole Earth Catalog, and the set was surrounded with model rockets, space ships and other apparatus that forms part of the permanent real estate of the Palace of Arts and Sciences; party-goers explored the adjacent Exploratorium, as the science museum is called, filled with an array of strobe environments, laser lights, optical illusion boxes, abstract television screens and other things dedicated to the alliance of art and science and the expansion of perception.

Occasionally, you would catch a strong whiff of weed, but it was notably rare considering the size and nature of the crowd. De rigueur clothing

121

ranged through several shades of casual—jeans and T/shirts, cords and sport-jackets, hotpants, maxis and minis—but there were scarcely any real costumes in the old Haight-Ashbury, Flower-Power sense of the word, even though the invitation had suggested, "you could come as a tool."

Perhaps people figured they *were* tools—tools of restoring balance with the land, of fashioning new means of mass communication, of revolution. The principal exception was Brand himself, barefooted and clad in a black monk's robe—a tool, perhaps, of the Lord's will, or perhaps, he was expressing renunciation of his entrepreneurial role in helping hold the Whole Earth together, or perhaps—well, what exactly did it mean?

A circle of seat-cushions filled the floor in front of an improvised stage with a resonant sound system, and at about 9:30 PM the show began: Professional clowns and trampoline artists, belly dancers, the Golden Toad playing Irish jigs and Tibetan temple music, even a Keystone Kops skit in which Brand was beseiged by uniformed fuzz reading a warrant charging him with defrauding the Internal Revenue Service and giving power to the Gods.

An undercurrent of expectation buzzed among people in the crowd who had noticed the fine print in the lower right hand corner of the invitation: "Attention Internal Revenue Service: this event is an educational occasion whose exact nature may not be revealed until 10 PM." Others obviously hadn't read that far, or they weren't concerned about it, and the volleyball and boffing beat out an insistent rhythm beneath the changing spectacles that held the center stage.

"Are you going to close the doors on everybody, at 10 o'clock, do another Liferaft Earth thing?" we asked Brand during a break at the "Demise."

"No, though it's a good idea. We'll do something. There's a hundred rumors, Take your choice."

Why the decision to fold the catalog at this particular point?

"We've done our job—provided access to tools," Brand said. "Among the choices of what we could have done, this seemed to me to make more sense than any others. It's the job you always try to do, to put yourself out of business."

Have the communities which the catalog was established to serve become stronger, more soundly based, during the catalog's three year period?

"They're learning fast. As near as I can tell, that's what they're for," Brand said. "In the communities, mistakes show immediately and they're consequential. They're the kinds of consequences that schools shield people from."

"The communities have become less serious, rather than more serious, in some ways, and that's why they're better," Brand added. "Traditionally, the most failures have been among the serious ones, the ones with great Utopian ideas who think they are going to do something spectacular and change the whole world. The stronger communities are kind of frivolous."

How much did the Demise celebration cost?

"I guess we have to continue to keep the costs out front. It runs to about $6,000. Some for the performers, a lot of it to keep the museum open as a functioning museum, with its entire staff working. Yes, it's a wake. I thought we might as well stop with a flourish."

At around 10:30 PM, the "exact nature" of the educational event was "revealed" in a fell stroke of Brandian genius that at once made everything fall into place—well, almost into place. Brand, who had spent the last three years providing the movement with access to tools, was now presenting it with the heaviest tool of all—money, precisely $20,000 in $100 bills—about the amount, Brand later explained, that he used to launch the Whole Earth Catalog.

The announcement, made by MC Scott Beach, abruptly stopped the more or less aimless party activity, meandering and chatter. "About 15 minutes ago, Stewart Brand gave me one of the tools that the Whole Earth catalog has used. This is $20,000, and he gave it to the people here to be used as a tool . . ."

Certainly the initial reaction of many was that the money would be distributed among the crowd, divided equally or in some other way passed out. Then came the rest of the announcement . . . "Use this as a seed. The Whole Earth Catalog ceases. The seeds have been planted already. Your consensus will decide what will be done with this money. There are microphones, there are causes, there are lots of possibilities."

The announcement produced two simultaneous jolts. For one thing, it instantly galvanized the crowd, or much of it, into a close-knit community of individuals joined together in a common purpose; it transformed the county fair into a New England town meeting.

The other reaction was a kind of apprehension that nothing was going to come of the whole thing. You just don't get 1500 people to agree on a single cause, especially where lots of bread is concerned, even 1500 people who might see themselves as crew members aboard some kind of Noah's Ark designed to preserve the treasures of civilization and human values from the flood-waters of ignorance and self-seeking destructiveness.

A parade of no less than 55 speakers filed past the microphones during the next hour, each holding for a moment the work of money as they presented every conceivable proposal. It should go to the Exploratorium, to the performers, to free political prisoners, to help the Indians, to buy land, to set up a free loan company, to put the Whole Earth Catalog on the shelves of high schools, to start a toy factory, to help stop high rises and strip mining; some of it should go to us, because our commune needs a new pump, or because we want to establish a radio station which we'll eventually turn over to minority groups. About half the speakers felt the money should go to projects they were personally involved in; the other half suggested schemes that ranged from plans to spray grass seed throughout California to a proposal to put on a world-wide Whole Earth party. Clad in his cassock, Brand stood on stage and noted each suggestion on a blackboard. At one point, a girl in the audience interrupted a speaker with the cry, "Free Political Prisoners," and Brand duly wrote it down; when she interrupted the following speaker the same way, he added an exclamation point.

It was difficult to tell what he thought of the proceedings. He was possibly pleased at the number of ideas that came forth from the speakers. He was clearly enjoying the study in group dynamics that the proceedings had launched. Was he expecting someone to come up with an abrupt flash of genius, a project that would seem so absolutely right that the entire crowd would suddenly stand united behind it? Was he simply watching everybody squirm, unable to cope with the curve ball he had thrown them?

The sentiment arose in at least one faction of the crowd that it had become a tool, that Brand had presented it with the Apple of Temptation. One speaker suggested that the money be flushed down the six johns provided for the Demise; others proposed that the bills be burned in the fireplace, or buried underground throughout the country and used as symbolic bait in a computerized Easter Egg Hunt. "Throw it to the crowd!" a few chanted sporadically.

Occasionally Brand stepped to the microphone to respond to this rising mood of ugliness. "How can we expect anyone else in the world to reach an agreement if we can't?" he asked. "Whatever we agree upon isn't meant to exclude anything else."

But firecrackers zipped above the stage, the number of volley ball players increased and the people seated in front of the stage began to drift away. Whatever else it did or did not do, it became apparent the the introduction of money on the scene had produced a bummer. As one spectator commented, "It took him $6,000 to put the party on, and $20,000 to spoil it."

At 11:30 PM, as no strongly exciting proposal had set the crowd afire, one man came to the microphone to suggest that everybody take a half-hour music break. A country-western protest singer from Vancouver held the stage for a while, and the Golden Toad returned for a hot set of Irish jigs.

When the crowd reconvened at 12:15, a few new suggestions were made, and then a man named Michael Kaye announced that the real problem was not *what* to do with the money—all the suggestions were sound—but *how* to give it away, and he and some friends of his were taking the responsibility to give it away then and there. "If you don't need this money, give it back," he said, and MC Scott Beach suggested that those who were taking the money should come to the microphone and announce the purpose they were taking it for. Much of the money came back, after Stewart pointed out that a large single amount of money was more powerful than small bundles.

The crowd was starting to thin and suggestions were slowing down. There seemed a tension between those who wanted to get the money for some project of their own, those who wanted to give it to some political cause, such as the Indians, and those who wanted to show their contempt for money by destroying it. No consensus was being reached. "The problem has got to hang for us," said Brand, "until we work through it."

Beach announced that the total amount of money in hand was now $14,200, counting what had been returned.

The man who had given money away took the mike and suggested that people who had taken money for personal reasons alone should give it back. Later the total rose to $15,100.

A familiar note in parliamentary proceedings was struck around 2:15 when a man took the mike and announced that the problem was to *make a decision on how to go about deciding.* A forceful young man with a moustache took over and got a consensus by voice vote that the criteria for an acceptable project should include that the project be on-going, self-supporting and self-perpetuating.

Then things fell apart again and it was suggested that the crowd, down to perhaps 350 by this time, might get more together if everyone held hands and breathed deeply together in what the Hog Farm calls a "Gong Bong." A mass Gong Bong was held. After breathing together for a while, and reassembly, there was a move to consult the *I Ching*. Paul Krassner had taken over from Scott Beach by this time, and he read the first symbol he opened to in the book, Hexagram 53, "Development (Gradual Progress)": "The Wild Goose gradually draws near the tree. Perhaps it will find a flat branch. No blame." The Judgment suggested that in inappropriate situations, it behooves a man to be sensible and yielding. "A believer should be doing this," said Krassner as he stumbled through the reading.

About 3 AM, a young man with wavy hair and a beard and an intense, earnest expression came to the stage and read a statement to the effect that the learning process that was going on here was more important than what would happen to the money. It was decided that eliminations would be taken among the suggested projects. "Groan your consensus," said Krassner.

The list was groaned down to: A trust fund, to be administered by San Francisco's Glide Foundation; giving the money to the Indians; some kind of communications project, radio or print; ecological business; and schools projects. Finally it went down to communications and Indians and seemed to deadlock there.

Another man spoke to the mood of frustration, suggesting that the money should not be spent at all. "It seems to me we're using old structures here, while we're trying to build a new world. We're using logical structures for an irrational situation. None of these suggestions really peaks us, and we can't decide among them.

"What we've learned tonight from this process is really heavy. Stewart has shown us just what a bunch of shit money really is. Let's *enshrine* this money as Stewart's lesson to us." The crowd was down to about 150 people now and it was nearly 4 in the morning.

"Think of what it would do to people's minds if there was this money that could not be spent. And then let's get it out here next year and get our heads bugged again. Maybe we'll spend some of it, but it will probably last ten years." There was a round of applause, the most enthusiastic response in hours.

Paul Krassner thought maybe they could just *say* it's been enshrined and really use it: It would be difficult to explain this enshrinement to the Indians. Also, he suggested, people's minds "may just not be as blown by this gesture as we imagined." A girl came to the mike and opined that America *already* enshrines money.

At 4:30, a compromise was suggested: part of the money should be given to the Indians, and part of it should lie untouched. This seemed to be acceptable to the Indian partisans, and to the communications people if they got a cut: but the people who were not for spending it were inflexible. Their position depended on making a statement with the whole sum.

The next round of applause came for the suggestion, "Let's wait a year and get better at being gods." A vote was taken and 44 hands were raised for spending the money, and 44 for not spending it. A new vote was asked for—the audience was to move to either one side or the other of the stage. Someone objected that this was the definition of separation. Those who were against dividedness asked to stand in the middle.

"We should get rid of the money, we're all too crazy to decide what to do with it," said one man. Another got a decisive round of applause for the proposal that the money be given "to an Indian, any Indian." An Indian lady was found, and she squealed with delight and ran up to the stage. But she had to announce that the money would lead to domestic conflict, since she was Stewart Brand's wife Lois, a full-blooded Ottawa.

The wavy-haired man who had spoken of the unimportance of money now came to the mike and read a petition he had started to pass around. He said, "The rule here is that we have to decide what to do with the money. But humans are greater than rules. People are more important than money. Money should be our servant." His petition read, in part, "We feel the union of people here tonight is more important than money, a greater resource." He asked people who agreed with him to sign their names and put down their addresses so that their meeting could bear fruit.

There was a move to give the money back to Stewart, the objection being that he was, as a fiction, "gone"—although he was still on the stage. "Gone," said Brand vehemently, "that's a good idea," as he walked from the stage and removed his monk's robes.

It was now after 6 AM and the sky was quite light outside. The crowd was down to about 40 persons, and it was decided that the podium and microphones were no longer necessary. The crowd gathered into a tribal huddle. A new suggestion was proposed that would solve everything: we should use the $15,000 to start the Whole Earth Catalog again. Stewart Brand and some of the Whole Earth people were already sweeping the floors, gathering up pillows and readying the hall for a return to Exploration use.

At 7 AM, Les Rosen of the Portola Institute told people the party was over. Many left, but a knot of about 20 people stayed outside the hall, The man with wavy hair who had been passing around the petition came back with a proposal that favored "developing people (our energy, ideas and friendships) resources for information, communications and educational networks." It was decided that he would put the money in a bank for a month and then reconvene the remaining 20 people to decide what to do with it. The total amount the man received—his name turned out to be Fredrick L. Moore—was $14,905 (apparently some money was pocketed during the early morning hours, but where the $5 came from remains a mystery).

Moore seemed to get the money by default, by persistence. Signing the money over to him was an anti-climax after the nine-hour parliament, done by a tired Stewart Brand on top of a pile of cardboard boxes. Moore wandered around for a while, bewildered and awed, trying to get riders to accompany him back to Palo Alto and wondering aloud whether he should deposit the money in a night bank deposit . . . then realizing he had no bank account.

At this uncertain point, the "community" of catalog makers may not have another chance to reach an agreement on what to do with the remaining portion of Brand's "seed" money. But Brand's parting flourish graphically laid down the next lesson it has to learn, the next initiation rite, perhaps even a new phase in the movement's continuing process of self-education. It is that money is neither God nor demon, but simply another tool, albeit the heaviest, and one which many people have ignored in hopes it would go away. At the Demise, it almost did.

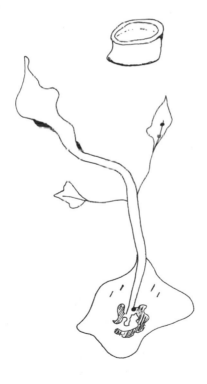

Destination-Crisis Paper for the POINT Board of Directors
Submitted December 3, 1971, by Stewart Brand

"What is most worth doing now?" is how I interpret the subject of Destination Crisis. The contractor for this paper and the target for recommendations is the nascent foundation POINT. Therefore: "What is most worth doing now with POINT's resources, namely the founding directors and staff, the cash surplus from *Whole Earth Catalog* sales, our non-profit foundation status, and, um, the world?"

The destination question also bugs our nation these days, and many an individual. (The prospect of planetary projects should be dragged in here too, but so far planetary consciousness is incoherent.)

René Dubos says that general panic in the years before 1000 AD was not so different from what we have now as 2000 AD approaches. What I wonder is, how were things in, say, 1002? Did people finally sigh, look around, and realize that nothing special was going to happen, that they were stuck with this world?

I suspect it was a healthy time, and I expect a taste of it shortly for America, who is only now—with Vietnam—walking from the Victory Dream of World War II. We can't save (control) the world, and so we are obliged to notice it.

My hope is that America will become curmudgeonly, as Wendell Berry or Steve Baer are curmudgeons. A nation skeptical, husbanding of resources, bitter defender of individual rights, impolite self-critic, with the mad gleam in the eye of the inventor. Slow to laugh, and slow to stop laughing.

In this way, maybe, America can grow larger than its power and teach it to be useful. In the individual, a reliable indicator of power larger than the person is good old Tremor of Intent. The poor soul wants to do everything Good and do it Right, and is defeated by overwhelming possibility. He is an easy mark for reformers, for abandonment to the single all-embracing Cause.

Yas, yas.
So much to know, so little time.
So much to do, so little time.
So much breath, so much whine.

To make the connection: "What should I do with $1,000,000?" is not very different from "What should I do with my life?" (If you could deal with only one question, which would you take?) We are blessed/cursed with the leisure, money, and access to try damn near anything we can conceive. Naturally this brings down enormous guilt—we see everywhere pain that we could buy the healing of. But—ah, but—experience shows us that external healing is usually temporary, and external help often hinders, and the false promise of cure is pure cruelty. So, idealists become pragmatists. (Some become cynics and depart from usefulness.)

Most pragmatists in time lose their joy amid the machinations of purpose, and their sense of value amid tangles of partial compromise. They abandon themselves to their projects until eventually there is nobody home.

Projects succeed or fail. Any observer of showbiz must note that fulfilled ambition is occasionally fatal. So is total frustration. What they have in common is the loss of the seeking self. Some projects are no doubt healthier than others—scientific research better than treasure-hunting maybe. But more central and determining is the conduct of the seeker. Scanning a quick array of useful current heroes sung and unsung, I noticed that the quality they have in common is integrity. Or, as the Hog Farm mottoes it, "Play Hard But Play Fair." These are the players who seem most capable of transcending win/lose while preserving their self *and* improving the game.

The only real fault I would find with most of the heroes is that they are over worked. Partly this is their own doing (more on leisure in a moment), partly it's simply due to the shortage of heroes. (Heroism is in scary repute these days because some who stood charismatically tall have been shot down. I believe they asked for it, some of them. They came to rely too completely on audience and visibility, until the vainglory showed and drew a bullet. If you sell your soul to the crowd, by and by they'll collect.)

It seems to me that the best solution to dead heroes and overworked heroes is not no heroes but more heroes. Spread the load. Spread the consciousness and skills of responsibility. (And, as they told us infantrymen, don't bunch up all the time, you're too tempting a target.)

The genesis and employment of heroes might be feasible. Damn near everyone, in this society anyhow, wants purpose, plot, and at least the possibility of audience. People will go along with almost anything that provides these for them, and eventually scuttle any scheme that denies them their own personal dramatic story.

(I notice that I'm going along with Robert Ardrey's proposition that the three main human drives are for identity, stimulation, and security—in that order. The desire to live a story comes under identity.) Dick Raymond favors fostering effective new traditions. In the hero department we have had for years the tradition of the hero from the ranks, he Establishment darling. This was the unlikely but plucky lad or unlikely but crafty old guy who rose to the occasion when circumstances and a desperate nation said "You! Handle it!" And we've had the tradition of the rebel hero who stood firm through the crowd's insults and bosses' deceits to finally BEAT city hall, and then quietly left the victory celebration to catch a ride on the evening freight. And sundry others.

Among the storied heroes I can't recall one who studied up and carefully selected his crisis. Yet most of our real-life heroes do precisely this.

To blurt out the "agency" scheme early on here, I wonder if we can nurture a demanding tradition for the subtle heroes.

Imagine, please, that POINT sets in motion a, hm, Peripheral Intelligence Agency (PIA), which employs Free Agents, at, say, $10,000/year with a $5,000 working budget. The Agents are hired for their resourcefulness at doing maximum good with minimum expenditure. That's minimum expenditure not only of money but of external influence generally—of personal pain, of entangling obligations, of extraneous meddling, of all the baggage that commonly clutters and defers good-doing.

The Agents select their own missions and carry them out their own way. Besides gainful employment and a modest budget, PIA offers only evaluation and information. Evaluation, through the full-time Board of Review in the form of comment and satirically pompous awards. Information, about potential missions, nuances of Agent technique, and whatever else proves useful.

What Agents owe the PIA is: to do elegant good (not suave or polished good, but *spare* good, fucking austere good), and to report on everything they attempt. Clearly the most significant managerial matter for PIA is deciding *who* shall be Agents. The hiring process might be sophisticated by putting prospective Agents through a one-month-$1000 trial period. Some persons with independent income may wish to be Agents-without-salary, and they should be provided for. In general I would expect most of the Free Agents to be in their thirties or forties, with a few younger and a few older. Employment should be for one year at a time, with only very exceptional Agents retained for a second or third year.

Elitist hiring like this can only be explained by the near impossiblity of really doing good, and only justified by actual undeniable good done. If PIA does nothing special, then it had better melt back into the pot. (There should be formal provisions for this.)

A major reason for structuring the Agency this way is to avoid or offset the tendency of most foundations to become wishful and sloppy, tightass in the world and looseass internally, and finally detrimental. (Glide Foundation appears to be a warming exception; are there others?) I believe that POINT should avoid the whole jivey hustle of grantsmanship and simply award no grants. All projects are internally initiated. A group that asks for help might well get help, but not money; an Agent they get, if he's interested (or if *she's* interested) and they want him (*her*).

(No doubt POINT will do some half-assed granting, and no doubt Agents will spend much time jivey hustling other foundations. All we can do is deplore it, discourage it, and try to keep it human. Who the hell wants a crew of very well funded cynics?)

I've thought about the proposal of searching out effective do-gooders in the world and rewarding them where they stand. What seems to happen then is they start doing rewards instead of doing good. I think they're better off left to their local rewards. Or, if they and we really want to get together, Free Agent employment could be a clean way to do it.

Here's some speculation on how an Agent might work. Free Agent Pete Bog is onto solar energy conversion. His Agent's report for November might include:

An insulting letter to Steve Baer to egg him on past Harold Hay's clunky insulation barrier apparatus;

A luncheon for Day Charoudi and Don Aitken to see if John Muir Institute could fund Day's solar biosphere research;

A phone call to Nowels' Printing to score free roll-ends for Day's heat-storage soup;

Forwarding a little-known report on the wastage of solar energy in urban environments to columnist Nicholas Von Hoffman;

Four-day visit in Adelaide to encourage Australian contestants to enter MIT's solar energy contest (good chance that Aussie sophistication will humiliate the US engineers and thus stimulate federal support for solar research);

Phone call to George Young at Ballantine Books suggesting he pick up paper-back rights on *Direct Use of the Sun's Energy*;

Two days with Steve Durkee urging that his next book be a pure celebration of the sun;

Letter arranging for *Consumer Reports* to test a new commercial solar water heater and compare its costs with standard equipment;

Two-day visit in Utah dickering with a mining company to get free use of old mine shafts for heat storage research;

Three phone calls arranging for an underground video crew to record next spring's Solar Energy Conference;

And, as usual, a critique of research material that Agent Bog used during the month. (Making up a list like this is heavy motivation; now I want to do all the stuff listed, even the fictional items.)

I notice that most of the moves I have the solar Agent make are brokering moves, catalyst action between otherwise inert reagents, social bisociation. But that must be only one member of a very large set of subtle Agent tactics. Some might involve right timing, knowing *when* a situation is vulnerable to change. All certainly would require some clairvoyant (whole-seeing) sense of consequences—*the* horseshoe nail that would stop the war, *the* troubling question for the research. One general strategy that I wholeheartedly buy from Fuller takes note of the folly of trying vainly to remove something when all you have to do is introduce something which obsolesces it.

(Incidentally, I have no commitment to change as panacea. In fact, the real goal is continuity, which is a kind of stability. The splendid evolutionary paradox is that continuity requires constant sensitive readjustment— not only change but precise change.)I think that POINT, like the *Catalog,* should be as transparent as any guppy—report fully on all its doings. One, it's nicer; it opens and warms many a channel of trust and communication, and it discourages the entire spectrum of blackmail. Two, it obliges us formally to notice what we are doing and how badly we are doing it. Three, we have a shot at informing and encouraging change-agents far beyond our poor gallery.

I just read in a film proposal by Ben Van Meter that "valor, honesty, integrity and patience formed the basis of Bushido (the code of ethical rules which the Samurai followed)." If the Free Agents could develop and live up to such an ethical code, it could be POINT's most seductive contribution.

Ken Kesey last night advised me to use the POINT money to buy corn (which is cheap this year) and a ship to carry it directly from here to the hungry and cut through for once all the obstructing bullshit, or at least spotlight it for what it is. Ken pointed with admiration at the present karmic

state of UNICEF's Danny Kaye. He quoted Don Juan's observation at the present karmic state, all roads are the same but
some roads have heart. Ken noted that the few times he had
given profound oracular advice was when he was in a state
of wanting nothing from the person asking.

The difference between compassion and guilt must be
the most important difference there is in the do-good business. Guilt shrivels, it wants something; compassion expands
far beyond the gift. I don't think we're ready to handle the
corn-ship right. But a year or so of ethical and operational
practice on the heart roads might get us in shape for big
league plays like that.

Learning heart technique requires a balance of work and
leisure, I'm convinced. Witness the Demise Party. (The
$20,000 surprise giveaway led to no original ideas and no
decisions; $15,000 announced giveaway six months later led
to good ideas and good decision; people had taken thought.)

In crisis we fall back on simplistic notions and old contingency plans. With leisure comes some return to the whole,
some chance to build different perspectives, new contingency
ideas, some reservoir of energy to dance with crises instead
of just survive them. Freedom, reverence, and creativity
come together.

Therefore, I suggest that whatever form POINT takes,
we see to it that all employees get three months of paid vacation a year. Also that nobody can remain continuously
employed by POINT for longer than three years without at
least a year off (unpaid) doing something else.

And I think we should fire people, maybe a lot. This can
only be useful if there is a clear shared sense of what con-
stitutes good work. Again, this is to avoid standard foundation behavior which encourages in-house dependents, Peter
Principle heaven, where every position is occupied by a fully
ripe incompetent. Firing is a good deal more honest than the
usual pressuring-out system, and is commonly good experience for the firee (cliché but true). The Greeks made ostra-
cism work very well; they'd kick out their faltering profes-
sionals and hire them back a few years later reinvigorated.
No position in POINT should be exempt from swift kick-out
accessibility.

I've tried to imagine what characteristics the most effective Free Agents would have, and haven't got far with it. I think we'll have to find out.

I have tentatively cataloged some elegance measures for evaluating missions and tatics. A good mission might be:

Regenerative — effects live on self-sustainingly

Expanding — cascading benefits, increasing sophistication

Adaptable — locally in time; exportable

Independent — not personality-bound or external-support-bound

Stable — self-correcting

Reality-based — e.g., in real self-interest of all involved

Locale-fitted — uses local resources, avoids local hazards, not threateningly exotic

Self-fitted — elements are mutually enhancing

Cheap/funky — satisfying rather than optimizing

Soft — or, if hard, then fast, or internal

Brilliant — unobvious solution

Original — our bit for state-of-the-art

Otherwise unlikely — If we don't lend a hand it probably won't happen (this eliminates many good ideas, which turn out to be happening anyway)

Successful — it worked

Obviously our Board of Review has some work ahead of it devising an explicit and evolving set of criteria for judgement. The "success" gradient is not too hard; evaluating "goodness" will be considerably more tricky.

The way I reviewed the success of the Demise Party Money Thing was by output levels. 1) If the game was well-enough wrought that it would go on a long time and yield hard lessons; 2) If good ideas and a good decision came out; 3) If the form were adopted by others, and 4) If it worked for them; 5) If the form developed a life of its own. Demise only reached level one, an interesting failure. Fuller's domes occupy level four and threaten to five. LSD is pure five ('goodness' still in question).

What POINT will eventually be good at and good for requires foreknowledge of evolution, which is exactly impossible. What we may know is where to begin. I suggest we use POINT to explore the humanitarian uses of applied laziness, independence, rigor, humor, and transparency.

'Applied laziness' means that the amount of work doesn't matter. The amount of effect does. And the *quality* of effect is mystery aplenty to keep us hungry and foolish.

Stewart Brand
December 3, 1971

Stewart's updated comments on his "destination crisis" paper:

I am completely bored with the subject of free money after 2 years of it. I'm in a mode that I make it or spend it, but not give it away.

We never really tried the agent idea, I'm personally not sorry.

Stewart Brand
1973

This story is from a Sufi tale relayed to us by Michael the evening *The Seven Laws of Money* began, we call it . . .

FOOL'S GOLD

Hey
        Little Girl
                Lovely Lady
Ever hear of the fool and his gold—that's me
You see, I'm
       not from your country
I come from a small kingdom very far from here and that's my home even if I never touch it again before I die.

It's something else—you and me together under one sun, we could both of us be poor as the salt of the earth and yet
                                 I know us
            to be rich
                unto
                    untold
                        riches

Listen here, how can you want what you know not, how can you know what you have not, how can you have it and not want it?

Listen, gold is a burden. Why? Because you must know it and you must want it before you can have it. Look at the miser, in a prison of his own making—counting his horde of coins behind locked doors, what would he want if he had it? All the world to know how rich he is—that's what he WOULD want—that's the temptation the Devil in him won't let go—he's always got to be secret. But the Tempter holds a vision in his eye, same as anybody else, and the miser sees all his neighbors, he sees it, all his neighbors staring at him, his gold, and

How they envy him now!

Um. No, not for me. If the price of gold is my single mind, then I'll be content to let it flow through my hands whenever and wherever I get the chance.

See now, the miser lives on top of the tallest building in the kingdom, on top of a stone tower and every day he conducts business and then he goes

---

Jug

                                up and up
and closes all the seven gates and each gate has seven locks
                                        and counts his coins
                                                gold and silver
and then he counts it again and figures how much more he has over what
he had yesterday.

    Does he smile now? laugh? or sing? No, not the miser, because how
does he know if he has enough? Pretty soon he might walk to the window, one small window he has in his tower room, and he might lean out,
lean out into the starry night and say

          Great Big Mirror in the Sky—

          Who is the richest man alive?

    Just then, night after night, this is the way it happened:

    Laughter rising from below, a slow-startin' hard-comin' bellowin' kind
of a laugh—it's the Fool, it's the Fool wandering drunk through the all tore
up patch behind the miser's place, the Fool has a shack there, that's where
he sleeps, at least sometimes, long as anybody can remember, he's head-
ing for the shack now, but first he stops to give a piss into the bushes
before he stretches out for the night and he sang a song, says something
like this:

          What a Fool am I
          A fortune in gold and silver hand-me-downs
          And
          (just in case today
          I might die)
          I spent it all last night in town.

    Then the Fool, he might usually laugh some more all the way into the
sack, and the miser up above, when he heard this, he'd slam his window
shut, sink deep into a pot boiling rage, and couldn't sleep nor all night
that night nor all day the next day,

    Well the miser conducted his business that day and then he retired
to his tower room to count his money and no matter how hard he tried,
it never came out enough, and he walked to the window, the one small
window in his tower room and leaned out into the starry night, and he
said:

          Great Big Mirror in the Sky—

          Who is the richest man alive?

Again he heard that slow-startin' hard-comin-bellowin kind of a laugh from down below and again the Fool stopped to take a leak and he sang, just as the night before

What a Fool am I
A fortune in gold and silver hand-me-downs
And (just in case today I might die)
I spent it all last night in town.

So, for two nights running, the miser got no sleep, fuming and fussing all night long.

The next morning he called his man and said,

"I want you to evict that damn fool lives in the shack behind. I want him out by tonight."

"Sir, you cannot evict him because you do not own the place where he lives."

"What!" said the miser. "If I did not own it, you should have foreclosed the mortgage or bought it up for back taxes!"

"But Sir, I could not, because the place where he lives is public land."

The miser almost smiled. "Then we have him. Go and have the Sheriff to drop by his shack with warning if the Fool does not move out his shack today, it will be bulldozed tomorrow.

Yes, Sir, said the man, and the miser gave his man a bag of gold coins.

"Here", he said, "give this to the Sheriff, and keep my name out of it. And, listen, you sorry two leg dog, have a bulldozer to stand by tonight, just in case."

The man went and told the Sheriff and gave him the gold coins and found the bulldozer and told the bulldozer operator where to be and told him that he would show him what he was to hit when he got there, and when he got the word from the miser, he was to go ahead and hit it.

Then the miser's man returned and reported all that had happened.

"What use are you to me?" said the miser. "I have to do all the thinking myself anyway. You're fired, as of now!"

Having dismissed his man for the last time, the old skinflint thought to himself,

"That's enough business for one day."

And he yawned and went up into his tower room and sat down at his table to start counting, but straight away he fell into a deep sleep, his head resting between a fortune in gold on his right hand and a fortune in silver on his left, and as the miser slept, his man, leaving the tower, met the bulldozer operator outside on the street, and the bulldozer operator wanted to know what he was supposed to hit, so the man pointed to the miser's tower and said

"That's it!"

and went on his way that was made for him alone.

139

Fools's Peace

Meanwhile the sheriff hunted up the fool at the palace shooting pool. "Unless you can produce a deed of title to your place, the fact is you're camping on public land."

The fool took his time, studying the table, but a cousin standing there has got to state the obvious, he says, "I know you have a deed somewhere, man, because remember? We traded it more than once in a card game."

The fool took his shot, soft and sweet, and everybody straining to hear, said his calm clear peace, he said,

"Couldn't be but one of three places—in my coat, at my place, or. . . . no, no, I can't do that to the old man. . . ." and draws the sheriff to one side, and he said

"Look here, Sheriff, if I produce it that deed of title's gonna show but one thing . . . that . . . in other words that poor old man who lives in the tower in front, well I'm afraid his place is included with mine, I don't care for myself. If I can stay there, fine, or if I got to go, but he's a harmless old man, lived there years and years, for his sake, please let it be, pass it by this one time."

The sheriff said, "You know me, if it was up to me, wouldn't . . . nobody in this world would ever suffer pain or discomfort in any way, but the law is the law, and no one man has the right to change it."

"Well," said the fool, "at least go by and give that poor old man the bad news, could you do that sheriff? Because I don't have the heart to do it myself."

The fool returned to the game, thinking about that famous

First Law of Mechanics
("To every action, an equal and opposite reaction.")

Course the Fool went home that night and as usual singing and pissing away he woke the miser sitting dreaming at his table, rousted him to the window, his bloodshot eyes like two baked apples, he shook his fist and then he saw the bulldozer and yelled the operator to come ahead on, and the bulldozer revved, and up in the tower window the poor old miser nearly lost his mind, thought he heard a voice yelling "Jump Jump" even though the tower was strong enough couldn't touch it with no bulldozer. But most heavy on the miser's mind, when he come running out of the tower, what's he find? The Sheriff, wanting to be kind, left him a warning and an eviction notice, very polite in the choice of words, but it wasn't SUPPOSED to be there at all, was the miser's view and he just about never recovered from the sight of it. Plus the next morning, the Fool having heard all that transpired, sent the miser a letter by messenger and the letter gave the miser permission to live in his tower long as he's alive. Also word was going around that the Fool had won back the deed from his cousin in a card game that night before, and titles and deeds being such as they are, the miser took to waiting up every night to listen to the Fool sing, but he never more would open his window for fear the stars might sass him.

What's More

Things were happening all along whereby the King, being like most kings, was fond of pleasure and that included all kinds of baubles and gadgets, because the King kept many wives and each wife had many things, plus hunting and travel abroad, the young prince in Paris, all these enlightened the treasury until the King would borrow from the miser and the miser grew in power and influence, and the King spent all the silver and gold out of the country, work was hard to get and pitiful small, love wasn't paying at all, and the King took off for his hunting lodge in the hills, and stayed up there hunting and fishing with the palace guard, terrible tears in the many houses of his many wives.

Best thing to do is to leave it be, I realize that, but one day they came marching down the street and into his shack, and rousted the Fool. It was the Mamas, every Mama in town, why they were at the Fool's door, don't ask me, they were there and they said,

> "You they call the Fool
> Supposed to be wise above all
> Supposed to be
>   knowing secrets
>   outside and in
>   We want you
>   to do something
>   then. Any time any of us,

welcome to come up here and waste our lives away, now we need food, and we want our gold and silver back, we're giving you your chance."

The Fool made for the back door and out into the tore up patch to take his morning piss and he sang

> "God in Heaven!
>   Hear me!
>   Send me gold, send me silver
>   from on high!"

and he was praying like that—"Send me gold, send me silver"—when the miser heard him and went to his window and looked out.

> "God in Heaven!
>   Hear me!
>   Send me gold, send me silver
>   from on high!"

A strange thing came to pass upon the miser's face, a muscular arrangement that was like unto the breaking of ice in the Spring and then it was positively flowing like a stream, and it was a great big fiendish smile. It was a smile even the most specialest of all saints get but once or twice a day. It was that smile could run away into some of that sardonic laughter you sometimes up and die of. And the miser took a bag of gold, and dropped it—plop!—on the Fool's head, slid off and dropped to the ground behind him.

Now the Fool is called the Fool for many reasons, one is he knows how to play dumb, and dumb is how he played it, he just scratched his nose, that bag of gold might have been a butterfly for all the attention it got, and the Fool kept on praying

> "God in Heaven!
> Hear me!
> Send me gold, send me silver
> from on high!"

The miser's eyes bugged out and he dropped his smile and grabbed two bags of gold and threw them hard as he could . . .

. . . and the Fool kept praying.

The miser began to laugh and laughing all out of control all the time throwing bags of gold and throwing bags of silver until he had thrown his entire fortune

away?

and himself half out the window, still laughing, tears out his eyes—my, my—

until at last the Fool zipped up his fly and said, sweet, and easy,

"Thank you Jesus"
and went inside and said to the Mamas,
"Go on out back and pick it up."
which when the miser sees it, comes to his senses, yells after the Fool
to stop them, and comes charging down out of his tower

too late.

The Mamas went with the gold, pausing only to give the Fool hugging and kissing on the way out, the gold's on the street now, it was a revolution or it wasn't, but all those that had noisemakers brought them out until it sounded like the Fourth of July in Arkansas. And the King, hiding in the hills, he heard it. And the miser, who was sitting in the Fool's shack crying his heart away telling his whole life story to the Fool was still waking up into the early afternoon poking around to find just one of those coins was all was on HIS mind, and finally he sits down and says,

"All I really want is a bottle of wine."
Comes a knock knock knock and two more
and two more at the door, hands extend a bottle of champagne and a voice
says

"From Mama with love."

Coming on top of that gold was already showering his head in the morning, the Fool was very self impressed, the Fool was, and he took a long draw at the jug before even thinking to pass it to the miser probably needed it even more, and the miser, he was deep into it before he left that night—
The Devil said

Drink

Ye

of this wine. I promise you to
feel fine

In the morning,

I will make the sun stop
Time stand still
Yes I will

The Devil said.

—and the miser was awful deep into it by the time he left that night, went up into his tower to jump out the window was his plan when one of his long time mignons came knocking at his door below, yelling

"Your Honor! Your Honor!
The King is back in the Palace!
Long live the King!"

started that poor old miser into thinking again.
The King, you see, had heard the snap, crackle and pop from up in the mountains. He turned to his right hand man and said,
"Let's go back to town and face the firing squad, I'd just as soon die as live and not be King."

Right hand man was no where.
The King turned and said
"Will you on my left hand go with me back into town?"
No answer.
And when the King turned all around, no one showed, so it came to pass the King returned to town a much wiser and improved upon man, all alone and unrecognized he slipped through the swarming crowds of his goldcrazed celebrating and carrying on subjects, just a little suprised at the going on's in the many houses of his many wives, all he said was

"When the Cat's Away"

143

But someone saw the King and word went around

"The King is back in the Palace!
Long live the King!"

And that's how the miser came to hear it and returned to find the Fool dozing bottle in hand.

"Wake up! Wake up my man, I would have words with you."

"Oh " said the Fool, "it's you. That's alright, you won't have to jump, I won't tell. Here, there's still a little left in the bottom of the bottle."

"No, no, no, no, no," said the miser. "The King is back in the Palace and I'm going to take this matter to Court right now for judgement and you're coming with me, if I have to . . . "

"Wait a minute, wait a minute,' said the Fool. "That's a long ways to walk in the middle of the night, sit down here and tell me all about it."

But the miser would neither tell nor show, he would insist. . . and insist. . .and insist until he offered to call upon his limousine to take them on up to Court.

What could the Fool say??

However, find out at this point—no driver. Sunrise poking over the horizon and the chauffeur still out playing around!

The miser said, "Alright, you drive."

"UmmUm. What's the King going to think if we come in your car and I as your chauffeur?"

So the miser drove the Fool to Court, and opened the door for the Fool and followed the Fool on into the throne room, still no guard, no minister, no flatterers and no caterers, just the King alone on his throne amidst all the finery, brooding over it, like the lone cloud of a starlit light. And here come two subjects of the realm, bow, and one says

"Your Majesty."
And the other says,
"Your Majesty."

The King shook his head and felt of the crown weighing on him and laughed himself a good two or three yards of laughter and the Fool, of course he starts in to laughing too, and then the miser sets in, and then the King stops and says,

"What you want?"

The miser was still laughing away on account he'd just got his start, so the Fool approached the throne and, off to the side, confided,

"No doubt you heard about the gold that fell from heaven last night, demonstrating that God is on your side, Your Majesty—and possibly saving your throne. This poor man that you see here fitfully laughing is suffering from the delusion that HE dropped all that gold from his window! A most pitiable condition, and yet harmless enough that, if you care to examine him, Your Majesty, I may perhaps suggest a kindly and yet effective disposition to this matter."

144

The King listened then to the miser, turned to the Fool, shook his head and said,

"I'm afraid you're right about this man. Perhaps he's lived alone too long. What was the disposition you had in mind?"

So he suggested to the King that

Give him IOU's for each and every gold and silver piece he thought he lost, the miser will still have something to count over long lonesome nights,

and the King (who already owed more IOU's to the miser than Peter owes to Paul) wrote them up and the miser used them for all his business establishments and soon, to make a long story short, today where there was once a fool's shack and a miser's tower you'll find a branch of the Bank of America and behind it a MacDonald's Hamburger Stand, and that's why I'll never see my homeland till I die, and that's why paper money is something I wouldn't wipe my nose on

you can have it . . .

make believe.

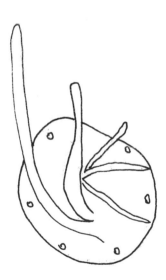

THE
SIXTH LAW

**You can never really receive
money as a gift.**

Money is either borrowed or lent or possibly invested. It is never given or received without those concepts implicit in it. Some people may say "Oh! I understand that, what you are really giving is Karma or receiving is Karma and Karma can be good or bad." Well, that's a possible interpretation. What I interpret this to mean is that the act or supposed act of giving money implies the creation of a "relationship;" It's a temporary imbalance. Giving money requires some repayment, if it's not repaid the nightmare elements enter into it.

Foundations learn that the kind of people who write good proposals and go asking for money are frequently the people who are incapable of doing anything once they have it; they are good askers, maybe because they don't understand what goes along with the money that is given to them, and the responsibilities. Maybe the Hope Diamond is an example of what giving things away is all about. I see many written foundation proposals from many different kinds of people over a long period of time. In my view, most of these people really ought to examine themselves. It seems that they become proposal writers and in the process of getting grants they become fictitious, imaginary people themselves. The process is highly destructive to them. Many people I know who have a great deal of money and have tried to give it away have found that it can't be done, that it creates as much of a burden to give it away as it does to keep it and that it is virtually impossible to give away because of the impact it has on the personality of the person doing the giving.

147

Not too long ago a group came to me and wanted to buy a gigantic piece of land. It was a group oriented around an Eastern religion and they naturally wanted to raise *money* for the gigantic piece of land. I said "You don't want money, you want supporters. You can go out and look for supporters and in the process ask for money, but don't forget what you're really after. Supporters." They did this. They contacted countless people, always asking for a small amount of money but in the process realizing that the commitment of a small amount of money was a commitment of support. And, of course, it was the support that built the institution and helped it grow. The institution is still growing. If this religious group had gotten a grant in the beginning it probably would have blown their whole future. Where would their supporters and friends and energy have come from, especially when the grants and funds began to run out in two or three years?

Remember the Second Law, which also applies to Law Six. When you get money, you've got to follow the Second Law, and you must deliver something for it. A gift of money is really a contract; it's really a repayable loan, and it requires performance and an accounting of performance that is satisfactory to the giver.

There are many ways in which the gift of money is not a gift at all, of course. It does destroy people's lives, as has happened to some Indian groups. I know of a free clinic that had done a spectacularly good job in San Francisco. It applied for a grant and was given an enormous sum of money. It virtually went out of business three weeks later as the whole group squabbled over what to do with the money and how to use it.

COMMENTARY ON THE SIXTH LAW

This Law sounds fairly harsh, but it is no more than the converse of the Fifth Law and embodies the same concepts of a loan, an alliance, and the long-term dynamic view of money.

There is a slight difference between the Fifth and Sixth Laws, just as there is a difference between a so-called giver and a receiver. The reciever plays more of a passive role and, like the heiress described earlier, the giver's action occasionally imposes a need for defensive reaction on the part of the receiver. Certainly such was the case for the woman in the Fifth Law who gave back her grant.

To some extent, thinking as I write about this vulnerability of the receiver and situations such as Lolly's generates a feeling of despair in me. Thinking about money, and money itself, has the power to evoke despair. Receiving money and the whole potential for despair in relation to money is the subject of this chapter.

Several years ago my father forwarded to me my share of an inheritance from a great uncle (Abraham Lincoln Phillips, a Shakesperian ham turned retail clothier who spent most of his 95 years in Petaluma, California, where my father's family settled in the 1850's.) My share was $500 after the inheritance was divided among my three younger brothers and me. I wrote my father and asked if he knew of any explicit or implicit expectations that my great uncle had concerning the money. My father took me seriously and remembered what this uncle used to jokingly tell him when he gave gifts of spending money: "Use it to pay the mortgage." That's exactly what I did with it. I was lucky; I knew the Sixth Law and acted decisively to find out the history of the money. If I hadn't had this background information I would have had to think seriously about what to do with the money, and the process of thinking about it could have been painful and revealing about myself, since it would have led me to deal with the money/despair issue openly. I would have had to choose between saving it or spending it on some possession. Saving would have led me to examine the question of why I save and what kind of protective money shield I was creating—protection from what? If instead I spent the money on a product, I would wonder who I needed to impress, what new need was I fabricating, and why? What kind of life-style was I driving at?

All these questions would have been generated by a gift of money. Money the psychiatrist? Yes, in a way. I see money as a mirror. An examination of your money and the way you use money is a way of understanding yourself in the same way that a mirror provides a way of seeing yourself. But, of course, because of the monsters that Freud found hiding within us we can be frightened, paralyzed and mortified by the mirror of money. It is commonly said that money is the root of all evil. This is a misphrasing of the original biblical translation "the *love* of money is the root of all evil." But who's to quibble when the mirror is such an easy thing to blame for what it reveals?

The monster/mirror quality of money became apparent to me a while back when I had a chance to see it in comparison to sex, a subject that clearly has intensity, fear and repression associated with it. For six months I was in a discussion group with eight men, counterpart to the women's consciousness groups. Once during those six months we brought up the subject of money and once we brought up the subject of homosexuality. In my own mind I know with certainty that the male fear of homosexuality is one of the most powerful cultural forces that influence our daily lives and our views of sexuality—yet it was so emotionally charged that we discussed it only for about an hour and politely went on to other subjects. Most of us felt we covered the subject adequately. Money we covered in only half an hour. Everyone politely described "the depths of his feelings" about money, and that was it. It's a subject so charged up that *we are often not conscious that we are not discussing it.* (What a sentence! But it says what I mean.)

I have strong feelings associated with money that have emerged in writing this book. I keep asking myself as I write why some of my dealings with money have been so painful.

You probably don't feel the same pain and agony while you're reading this. As I sit here writing, the pain takes the form of a personal depression that comes from saying "Help! What in the world is there for me to do? I'm worthless." It's the kind of depression that just sits there and stares at you—a sort of a gloom that implies there's a big hole inside of you, while you just sit and feel that enormous hole. Maybe it's like looking at your leg when you know it's about to be amputated; it embodies hopes on the one hand and memories on the other. I see the immediate present as some sort of transition which doesn't give me any confidence or feeling of security. Talking about the elements of money and examining them creates the feeling that money is tied to the whole universe. Maybe my feelings arise because we don't have the rituals surrounding money or writing about money that we have intertwined with religion, for example—rituals which allow us to deal with powerful forces and to derive some of the excitement, joy and ecstasy that come with rituals when they are applied to strong forces. Maybe the pain comes from writing about money, which is a non-logical, non-rational subject to begin with—money being experiential, almost hyper-experiential. Money governs experiences, yet it can't be experienced itself. In that sense it's like art. You can experience a painting directly by seeing it, but the "creative process" behind the painting is something the viewer can't experience.

Guilt plays an extremely powerful role in our relations to money. There are large numbers of people who feel that they have too much money, there are many who feel that "other people" have too much money, and there are many who sometimes feel that they have devoted too much of their lives to seeking money. This is a reflection of guilt and money.

Guilt also plays an important role in many forms of giving and consequently in receiving. Of all the forms of charity, direct giving provides a good example of guilt (like giving to the Red Cross for food packages, giving aid to victims of an earthquake or to women who are the victims of rape after a revolution.) When giving is direct and deals with personal guilt, people pour the money out. Their feelings of guilt are sometimes of such a quality that enormous quantities of useless material are amassed. Almost every time there's a disaster people bring their food and clothing to the Red Cross, and usually the Red Cross can't do a thing with them. It would cost much more to ship used clothes and dented food cans to victims of a disaster (who usually don't wear our kind of clothes and don't eat our kind of food) than it would cost to buy the equivalent items in an adjacent country. And yet the food and clothing pour in.

The more I think about guilt in writing this, and the more I talk about it with Salli, the more important I feel it is to describe its connection with money.

After trying some of the more conventional and psychological ways of looking at the money/guilt association and failing to be satisfied with the ideas, we turned to the *I Ching*, which gave us number 62: "*The Preponderance of the Small.*" In the judgement section it says:

"*Preponderance of the small--success, preseverance furthers, small things may be done, great things should not be done. The flying bird brings the message. It is not well to strive upward. It is well to remain below great good fortune.*"

The interpretation section says:

"Exceptional modesty and conscientiousness are sure to be rewarded with success. However, if a man is not to throw himself away, it is important they should not become empty form and subservients, but combined always with a correct dignity and personal behavior. We must understand the demands of the time in order to find the necessary offset for its deficiencies and damages. In any event, we must not count on great success, since the requisite strength is lacking. In this lies the importance of the message that one should not strive after lofty things but hold to lowly things".

The image that the *I Ching* gave is: "*Thunder in the Mountain.*"

"*The image of preponderance of the small; thus in his conduct the superior man gives preponderance to reverence, in bereavement he gives preponderance to grief, in his expenditures, he gives preponderance to thrift. Thunder on the mountain is different from thunder on the plain. In the mountain thunder seems much nearer. Outside the mountains it is less audible than the thunder of an ordinary storm. Thus the superior man derives an imperative from this image. He must always fix his eyes more closely and directly on duty than does the ordinary man, even though this might make his behavior seem petty to the outside world. He is exceptionally conscientious in his actions. In bereavement, emotion means more to him than ceremoniousness, in all his personal expenditures, he is extremely simple and unpretentious. In comparison with a man of the masses, all this makes him stand out as exceptional, but the essential difference, the essential significance of his attitudes lies in the fact that in external matters he is on the side of the lowly*".

What does all this mean in terms of money and guilt? I think my personal interpretation helps to clear the message: If you are a lowly person, if you are really "together" (to use the current vernacular), you don't have any guilt. Guilt arises from not having fulfilled your personal expectations. The role of money, the mirror, is that it tells us who we are. When we feel guilty because we think there are poor people in the world (people poorer than we are), we associate this with money, because money is the conceptual connection that links us to the so-called poor. For example, parents in the United States perenially refer to "the poor people in China" who are hungry. This is really a way in which we use money to reflect something about ourselves. We react to the difference between the average amount of money people in each country earn, when the only real relationship between people in China and us is at a cosmic level. The real relation we have with them has nothing to do with the amount of money we have in our bank accounts or the amount that some Chinese have in yuans' worth of cattle.

The *I Ching* says *"In his expenditures, he gives preponderance to thrift."* My interpretation of this is that somehow guilt also comes from a sense of lack of control, of being a spendthrift, of not being able to handle ourselves. It is commonly said about money that it has the power to overcome us, to rule us, to take us out of orbit, to make us gamblers or drinkers, to make us work 23 hours a day so that we don't see our families. That is preposterous. Money can be tied to guilt only because of its mirror-like quality, its ability to present our lack of self-control to us.

Upward to the Seventh Law.

Salli

Why Elephants Don't Have Money

We needed to talk with Richard!

We interviewed him over grapefruit; or did he interview us? It was exciting to be with Michael and Richard, who are so deeply committed to right livelihood, these two men who work together, run together, try to figure it all out and pass on what they learn. Richard says he lives between the cracks. Michael says money will come to you if you are doing the right thing. Strange words from men involved with giving large sums of money.

We laughed a lot and argued a bit and philosophized, adding Richard's voice to the money book. We didn't tape ourselves; we took some notes and mostly remembered our morning together. In a rambly fashion, here are some of the things Richard had to say.

The original beauty of bartering has been lost, and there is a deep hunger in many of us for the re-invention of this original system of exchange. We are searching — for the essence of exchange, wishing to become more aware through participation in it. We know we have fallen from the garden. We have divided the original barter system into new ones full of holes. These divide, and there are more holes and more divisions, until a sieve is created. In paradise, there would be personalized money; our currency would be created by us all the shades of the rainbow.

People sense a need to go back somehow to their roots. Many flee the city thinking they can ignore money by returning to the land. They hope to recapture their gifts. Full of idealism, they attempt to remove the need to "get ahead"; their cry is "No more More". There can be no security in money, but to the person who fixes on attachments there will always be a need for more.

We do need to share value systems, help create the new world together, to re-examine ourselves. It is very difficult to live simply, very hard to return to the land. Is there a harder path than that of the idealist?

Richard wanted to have better money consciousness, so he wrote the following for the first issue of Portola Institute's *Briarpatch Review*.

> *Money, which represents the prose of life, and which is hardly spoken of in parlors without an apology, is, in its effect and laws, as beautiful as roses.*
>
> —*Ralph Waldo Emerson*

The subject of money seems to lead people down one of two tracks. Track A, which has been the most popular one throughout nearly all of recorded history, is called "Money is The Root Of All Evil." Track B, which is magnificently described above by Ralph Waldo Emerson, might be called the "Beauty of Roses" track. It isn't a very popular track these days.

Emerson's understanding of money arose from quite a different mind set from most people's. His extraordinary mind saw something, in other words, that few people then were prepared to understand: That money is a brilliantly conceived invention of humans, and only when its use is perverted is it the root of anything evil.

If this wise man's statement stabs painfully at your cherished dogmas about money, it may be a good moment to lock up your shop for several days and seek out a safe place to talk things through with yourself. To be sure, it is not recommended that your re-evaluation be done in public. As almost everyone realizes, the subject of money now out-ranks sex as the topic which most people have the greatest fear of discussing honestly, either privately or in public. And for decent people to appreciate money as "the beauty of roses" is grounds for manslaughter in most of the United States.

But for anyone who is unafraid and willing to begin with childishly simple questions, think for awhile about why elephants don't have any money, for example. (After 20 years as a practicing economist, that is the question I found myself embarrassingly asking myself recently—in private, of course.)

Four words are useful in explaining the non-pecuniary state of elephanthood: *wants* (as contrasted with) *needs*, *specialization*, and *intelligence*.

Very simple, because elephants are concerned only with food and physical survival, and because they have virtually identical skills, talents, and interests, there are very few favors they can exchange or want to exchange. Furthermore, if they did think of some ways to trade services, they probably aren't smart enough to think of keeping score with currency.

Or to put it differently, homo sapiens is curiously blessed (or burdened) with desires, with differentiated talents, and enough money to figure out efficient, durable systems to save effort and reduce boredom. Hence, any society of craving, skilled people will unavoidably invent a currency system.

So how does that lead to Track A and "The Root Of All Evil" dilemma?

To be moralistic, Emerson is right about the beauty of roses, if they are tended by a caring grower; similarly the money system, if it is to be a brilliant invention of human beings, depends upon a caring and well-informed society. Regrettably, in a society that encourages or tolerates greed, the money system (like an untended rose garden) can be perverted with astonishing ease.

The perversion is not wholly a moralistic issue, incidentally. The tragedy of money is also attributable to a gross lack of consciousness about two of the four words mentioned above: wants and needs.

Through a careless use of language for a long period of years (during which time, for example, advertisers and their executive seniors claim publicly that brunettes "need" a hair rinse that contains silicon-J) our culture has bent to such a degree that few Americans honestly understand the distinction between discretionary desires and primal needs.

The return to a consciousness of simple, selective wants may perhaps be one of the major contributions of the Briarpatch society to purifying the money system.

"E.C. Rider"

E.C. Rider, see what you have done
You love me Rider, now this other woman's come
Love me, Rider, now young woman's come
Rider, I give you all I earn
Now you tell me it's some other woman's turn

You left your woman, Rider
Now you're on the run
You left your woman, Rider
Now you're on the run
You left it, Rider, you let it go
Now, Rider,
>   don't
>   you
>   start
>   feelin'
>   low

E.C. Rider is the name, born here, got off last night of a freight train, of course I didn't know where I was, fog was thick as tear gas in Washington, D.C., I couldn't hardly walk and could hardly see, but I looked up to a roadsign and it said   This is
Your
Hometown

——wella wella wella better look around. E.C. Rider, but they have yet to make a road straight enough for me—not only did I fail the test but went on over the edge, tumbled down the cliff and landed on the beach below, compadres camping around a fire, one of them looked up and said
     "Let him sleep. We ain't got but about so much wine anyway".

The fire was down to about a cigar butt, time I woke up, and everybody was down except old big belly moon was up, and I listened all around, cause I heard somethin', of course I heard the surf poundin' and scrubbin' but I also could just about hear fresh water somewheres, a rocky stream, sounded like, and a big steaming waterfall, that's what I heard. I shook a leg on down the beach, rocky cliffs on my left and the ocean on the right hand until my feet felt fresh water, and walked right up that river bottom, crickets making a terrible sound every step of the way.

I heard the crickets and I heard the night, the waterfall roaring so loud in my ears now couldn't even hear the surf was way off awhisperin', and somethin' else to tell, I heard a singing of little voices and bells ringing, seemed from amongst the stars above, and when I stopped to look up at this, my eyes first cast upon the waterfall ahead and for just
         that

long, not a sound, and off the highest rock, silhouetted against that big belly moon, a fine young woman lithe as a willow rod, wet smooth and slick and shiny, Wham! She did dive off the rock and disappear into the basin of the falls, which was still upstream some twenty thirty yards, and all of it over my head.

You know, it put me in mind of what my Daddy told me as I was stepping out the door.

   "Son", he said, "Remember this and keep it in mind—not every pussy is for lickin'."

Daddy was right about that, and not only, but what IS for licking you're going to know it, cause it'll smell sweet as jasmine from across the room and outside the window, and when you brush up against it, it'll open up like a morning glory and by the time you're done it's going to stand up like a trumpet and gleam like glass. That's what I was memberin' all the time, while what I was thinkin' ahead was

—"E.C., I'm goin' to get me one of them. I'm goin' to stick out my fishing pole and haul one in". Whilst I was actually doing at the time, I was moving up and around the rim of the basin, nearing to the rock they were diving off of. Meanwhile the pussy was clamboring around those mossy slippery rocks, splashing and falling off into the water, a big mass of them like a ball of ants, and the sugar bowl, the mountain top, was the diving rock. You think about it, you'll naturally conclude the ones that reach the top will be the best—the cream of the cream, but I was just a little too far from it to make my move when I sniffed it, my tongue jumped (it was like coke only better, Daddy knew what he was talking about) but I must have either slipped or gone after it when it jumped because the last I remember was falling and when the sun rose in the morning, there I was on a little sandy beach next to the falls and I still could see her like she was—in sight and out of reach. Now listen, just then the Muse spoke to me, and you know what she said? She said,

   "What my Mama told me was, Daughter, look out for the turkey, that old bird is almost gone, and why? Because it's good eatin." That's what Mama told her.

Want to know what my Dad said when he died? On his deathbed he said

   "E.C., I've lived a great many years. And someday you'll have a few years under your belly too and just always, someday, try to remember—Grow old gracefully, don't always be chasin' after young pussy, take what comes your way and that's that".

That's what I thinking about in the morning so I shut my eyes to dream some more. You ever dream this? You're just nodding half awake and it's raining and everything is dark and green and when you look out the window it's raining real slow and silent. Something like a

       motion

---

waterfall and when you look at it, you see bodies dancing in the rain and they are the rain. And maybe at some later or even at some later date and in another mood you might almost see it and, if you're like me you might even go out into the rain and feel of it. I don't know why.

Anyway, that's probably something to do with the fact that I went under the waterfall and found the door, a small steel door like a hatch on a ship, and I opened it, and I stepped in. Total darkness, but there was something in there cause I heard it, and if there is a sound that if you hear it, you have HEARD it, that's it—you ever hear a rattler? I jumped back, backed out from under the falls quicker than the electrified monkey, but I couldn't sleep after that, cause I was almost sure, just something in my mind kept after me and came after me and stayed right with me, and that was the sniff I got as I was closing the hatch after me, because it just had to be, it just had to be—the same as the rattler had to be a rattler. I thought to myself

"Even old Adam in the Garden of Eden didn't have to go through this to get him his cherry."

I went back of course, although it took me some hours to muster my courage and by the time I did go back—under the water and through the hatch door— it was moonlight only and I was all alone and powerful hungry and as I stepped in, I remember, I couldn't smell a thing, just damp, and I stepped in real slow and I was thinking whether there might be something to eat in there and I felt for the wall, I remember that, but what I felt was

FLESH

my arm was pulsating with that what they call

TANTRIC ENERGY

flow

off of that flesh wall and through my spine like a thousand hits of Acid equalized in one wad—no way I could not reach for the sky and I

touched it!

Can you touch and feel it? I touched it, and it was flesh too, and the door closed behind me, Bam! And the flesh came for me and hands and mouths stripped my ass naked and then the same as it had come for me, the hands and mouth were gone, just could feel it in my feet under me, that was flesh too (wasn't no soggy belly either) it was belly dancing under my soles and heels and all over the floor, no way I could stay up, plus I wasn't trying to prove a thing but I was standing all the same, on account of the electricity, and then I sniffed it again, not only that but I sniffed it from below me and coming toward me until the first I felt of it was the tongue and the soft inner linings of the mouth and the pearly cold teeth and I couldn't tell you if it was tambourines or rattlers or what, all I know I grabbed ahold and did all I could, you won't believe it but it tasted sweet as honey.

Then comes the time, no not the first, but comes the time once and again and yet again, when we stop, and it's quiet and something in my brain is saying

Watch It

---

cause it was dark and couldn't see, no matter we being that close there was no need to see. Then it came, once and again and yet again, something moving over and around the love body that was both of us—something cold and clammy damp wet, come that yet again, I just thought to hear that rattler, but I thought it so bad I DID hear it, and when I jumped up, Baby, you're still holding on, got your legs around my ass and saying

Yes! Yes!

but I made for the hatch and sprung it and brought you out and you're fighting me

remember?

biting and

scratching to stay

inside until I had to pull you out until your fingers were covered with blood and there you sit, Honey, when that hatch slams to behind us and we're safe and sound in the Real World—and there you sit

your

head

hang down

and cry.

What can I tell you now that you know? I took her, took her by the hand and down the canyon and along that beach and up the shore and down the road and into town and hustled diamonds and gold and gave her the child growing inside and what more can a man do but make himself a fool?

At last I asked her, "Baby, what do you need? Baby, something is wrong, what do you need?"

And she said, "I want to go home!"

I took her then and by the hand back up that road, down the beach, and followed the fresh water to the waterfall, it was morning and the sun was shining, birds singing, I left her on that little sandy beach and went on under the water to find the door and look things over and it was gone! the door, there was no door, no traces or sign where it had been, just rock—and I scratched, damned near ruined my knife trying to find it.

Well, I came out from under the falls and you probably guess it already—she was gone.

Just as no sign of one nor of the other—no footsteps, no tracks, no trail, and I searched till sundown and then I kept on ahowlerin' all night like a coyote bayin' at the moon.

"Lord I don't know whether I was born too late or too soon."

In the morning I did fall
into some kind of sleep, and in the morning
somebody woke me, was a lone cowboy sitting on a horse, high up over the falls and squinting at me from under his big old gray Stetson.

"This is a warnin' ", he says. "The next time I catch you up here I promise you I will shoot and or run you in for trespassing. This is posted private property, Stranger."

Jug

I looked up at him and I didn't give a damn if I was to live or die, I said
"I want her back, I want her back. I'll give you, pay you, anything
you ask but I've got to have her back".
"Pay me?" he says, and he laughed and says
"Alright, you pay me
                        cash
                                coins
one of each and she's yours.
"I'll do it! I'll do it, Mister, I'll get your money for you!"
"Alright," he says, "but meanwhile until you do, and I want one of
each of every coin that ever was minted, and until you get the complete
collection, you just stay out of here or look for flyin' lead."
And he backed his horse away and disappeared somewhere up there and here
                        I
am and I sure would appreciate it if you'd just let me look through your
spare change and see if maybe some of the coins are ones I'm still missing—
it'd help me a lot
                    it
                sure
                    would.

THE
SEVENTH LAW

There are worlds without money.

I think it's important to keep in mind that there are possible worlds without money. When you're asleep and dreaming, that's a world without money. There may be other places in the universe, there may be other concepts and other states of life in which there's no money, but the last Law makes it really hard to forget that everything we do when we're awake is related to money. You can take it away, such as with people in prisoner of war camps; but cigarettes become money. It's there as long as there are people to interact and they are awake.

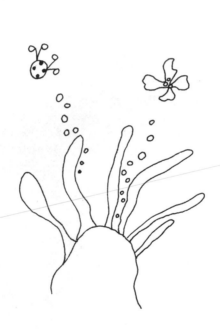

COMMENTARY ON THE SEVENTH LAW

This law has a little ironic twist to it, because what it says is that the world we live in is the world of money, and those of us who aren't willing to see it and deny the role of money will unfortunately be the ones for whom the world will be the least pleasant.

The history of man's creation of money isn't too clear, but it is fascinating. I got most of my information from Rupert J. Ederer's *The Evolution of Money* and Paul Einzig's *Primitive Money*. Man has apparently been a tool-using animal for several million years, but the period around 5,000 years ago when he began to domesticate animals was the first time rings and axes appear to have been used as exchange goods. These artifacts have been found in burial sites in Brittany, Crete, Mycenae and Silesia. By the time of the Pharaohs, 4,000 years ago, copper was used as the unit of exchange in Egypt. An alloy of copper, silver and gold was used in Babylonian, Indian, and Chinese coins. Hammurabi's code required merchants to accept silver in payment for commerce, and Egyptian granaries recorded their banking activities in the form of grain loans with interest.

A thousand years ago, the Chinese in the Tang Dynasty issued paper money, followed five hundred years ago by the development of banking and paper currency in Europe. (Curiously, the Jews seem to have been around the Middle East when coins emerged, and they were right on the scene when banking first developed in Northern Italy.)

Today money and the processes that are its visible qualities; interest, profit, capital, inflation, etc.—seem to be everywhere—in spite of the fact that there was no conference held to create it, there is no constitution to control it, and no advertising campaign carries it to the ends of the planet.

And yet the Seventh Law says that there are worlds without money. They are the worlds of art, poetry, music, dance, sex, etc. the essentials of human life. The Seventh Law should be like a star that is your guide. You know that you cannot live on the star; it is not physically a part of your life, but rather an aide to orientation. You are not going to reach this star, but in some sense neither are you going to reach your destination without it to guide you. The recognition of the role of money in your life from birth until the moment of your death comes from an understanding of where you are: it is where you walk and struggle and eat and think and understand. The star—the Seventh Law—is there to say that there is somewhere without money. You can't reach it except by focusing on the non-money parts of life—what you do, how you work, who you are, and who you associate with.

This is related to the famous statement that a fish could not discover water, or that Indians did not see "scenic vistas" as we modern tourists do. That there are worlds without money is a way of saying that a fish's life would be different if he could simply acknowledge that he does live in water, and the legendary Indian's life would have been different if he had realized that he lived in an environment that was mostly within the range of his eyesight. The star—the Seventh Law—is a way of saying that we are in the money, just as a fish is in the water, and that recognition of this can greatly influence how we respond to the world around us.

Epilogue

A great deal of agony is involved in writing a book, so I think it's only fair to offer the reader who might be curious an idea of why I was willing to spend the time and energy to write this book.

The history of *The Seven Laws of Money* is fairly straightforward. The original Seven Laws of Money were compiled in the form of a seven page "pamphlet" at the request of Salli Rasberry, who was working on a book concerned with free schools, called *Rasberry Exercises*. Salli wanted some information for people working in free schools to help them cope with the seemingly insurmountable problems surrounding money.

It happened that my friend Jug 'n' Candle was in town, and I mentioned to him the day before I was to be interviewed by Salli that she had asked me to talk about money. Jug, a poet, always seems to be in town when I need him. He said he'd be glad to help and proceeded to tell me about the concept of "seven laws," which comes from Tao philosophy. There are a number of sets of seven laws, like the Seven Laws of Travel and the Seven Laws of Prayer. He told me how you constructed them. He didn't lay out the whole process in advance, but instead led me to discover it. He said, "I'll tell you how to create the First Law and then you see if you can think of something about money that fits that description." I thought of it and told him. Then he told me how to create the Second Law once I had the first. I thought about it and came up with the Second Law. The Third Law was formed as a synthesis of the first two, the Fourth is its opposite, and so on.

We proceeded until I had done the Sixth Law. Then I asked Jug how to arrive at the Seventh Law. And he said "You can't arrive at it. It deals with something that you just can't arrive at." I said, "Oh, that sounds to me like—", and thereupon I laid out the Seventh Law. "Yea", he says, "That's what the Seventh Law is—that's the sort of conclusion you jump to when you realize you can't logically arrive

172

at the Seventh Law. It's like the question that is always on the end of a French doctoral thesis.

I then had the tape transcribed, typed and sent to Salli. Along the way some of my friends got copies. One in particular was Dick Raymond, who liked it so much he made some copies and started passing them around.

Within a few months I had more than a dozen requests from people around the United States—churches in Atlanta, executives at IBM in New York, etc. asking for copies of "The Seven Laws." Eventually a major publisher, Penguin, sent its West Coast Editor, Don Burns, with an offer of an advance to turn it into a book. I agreed to think about it, which I did. The only thing we settled on at that time was that if I offered the book to anybody it would be to Penguin, and that we would keep a record of our negotiations and discussions, which would be included in the book. (In the end Penguin's New York editors overruled Don and said no.)

As the book began to take form in my mind, a group of friends coalesced around a publishing organization called Word Wheel. My personal ties to Word Wheel went back a long way, to my membership on the Board of Portola Institute (I'm still on the Board after six years). Portola spawned *Big Rock Candy Mountain*, which published several educational journals and ultimately became Word Wheel. This made some sort of an alliance a natural thing.

It took three months for me to decide to do the book. My struggle had to do with reasons that are not necessarily obvious. I was not too interested in the money which could have come from the advance, nor fame, nor the desire to help people. My reason for not doing it in the beginning was that I had already written "The Seven Laws," and anything else seemed like it would be ineffective popularizing. Like the Sufi tale, in which the Murshid came into the classroom after the class had decided to ask him some terribly difficult question. "What is the meaning of life?" they all asked him at once, and he said "Which of you knows the answer?" No one raised his hand, so the Murshid said "In that case, you wouldn't understand it if I told you." The next day the students discussed the matter and came up with a solution.

173

When the Murshid walked in they asked him to tell what the meaning of life was, and he asked "How many of you know the answer?" They all raised their hands, and he said "In that case you certainly don't need to hear it from me." The third day they thought they really had him. He walked into the classroom and they asked him again the meaning of life. He once again asked "How many of you know the answer?" This time half the class raised their hands and the other half didn't. He said "Fine, now the half that knows can tell the half that doesn't."

Using this story as a model, I was highly reluctant to work for months to popularize what I had already done in a matter of seven pages.

Other things influenced me, however, and slowly changed my mind. There were discussions with Jug 'n' Candle which led me to think that I could possibly write a book that I would be interested in reading myself. Secondly, my mother said I should do it. She wanted a famous son. Her conception of fame was to be known within a certain elite circle of book readers, a friendly group of people to be famous among.

A strong additional reason, which is personal and not easy to say, is that on two occasions I have had failures in dealing with my views relating to money. Deciding to do the book was almost as though I had a desire to remedy those failures.

The first failure occurred after I left graduate study in economics in 1962 and decided that I had a unique economic theory which should be published. I finally wrote about 100 pages, which never got published. It was too long for a journal article. The distinct thing about the theory now, in 1974 is that its projections and hypotheses have all been tested and validated, and the theorems have all become their own distinct areas of economic study. To this day, however no one has published the core theory.

My second failure occurred when I was a banker. I had set out to discover ways to help managements of large corporations—those with at least $50 million dollars a year in sales—to become more efficient in using their money. I did

174

a very careful study, which involved talking to many corporate finance men. I looked at their daily operations and finally came up with a model of how to help them significantly improve their cash handling. The model was very simple, very powerful, and could be applied to almost every major company in the country; as of today it probably still applies to 95 out of a 100 companies. This was another situation like publishing my economic theory—the existing institution wouldn't respond. I had a hard time finding anybody who would even listen. The mystery that surrounds the management of money in large corporations is so great that people wouldn't listen to a 31-year-old banker saying "There's a very simple way to change what you are doing and save a lot of money."

I finally stumbled on two professors at Berkeley, in the Graduate School of Business, who had developed exactly the same model I had. They were no more successful than I was in finding interested corporations.

I was also reluctant to write a book because the current book format has two drawbacks. The first is that I don't think it has much of a future. Right now, looking to the future in the mid 70's, I feel that the current book format probably has only fifteen years to go. I am convinced that the computer-based information utility that we can see on the horizon will wholly replace the book as a source of information. Focusing so much of my energy on this current media made me uncomfortable. The way I plan to get around it is to put this book into a computer, in the hope that we can learn something well in advance of the information utility about how information is fed into a machine, how it is stored, how much it costs, who uses it, and what type of access people need. In general, I hope to learn from this experiment, where a book is put into a computer, what can be expected in the evolution of the storage of information—and to justify my current efforts.

The second thing I was concerned about was the "fictitious quality" of books, especially non-fiction ones. This quality can be seen in analogy to a zebra. A book is a discrete selection of information from our universe. The selection process almost compels you to treat the book's subject matter as a consistent whole. That's one of the implicit concepts of a book—it has a beginning and an end, and it covers the subject matter fairly extensively. Yet a book creates an aspect of reality that does not exist, in the same way that, concentrating on a zebra's blackness, the light colored stripes would be phased out of the foreground of perception, temporarily giving the picture of a black zebra. I've tried to counter this problem of focusing on reality through a limited viewpoint with drawings, photos, poetry, and other peoples' points of view.

The other part of the analogy between books and zebras is painting the zebra all white—which is essentially what an author does with himself in a book. Authors have a whole spectrum of characteristics, and from these characteristics, using his language and a certain select viewpoint, he chooses a picture of himself. It is almost inevitably all white, because he has the time to select the thing he wants to use to impress others. My experience with authors is that the ones I know are quite different from the pictures they create of themselves in their books.

Salli wants a better explanation of this last point, without the zebras. Well, in a narrative book you try to transmit a segment of your personal experiences. How can the readers view their experience out of context from your background and your motives? They can't, and I wanted to get them in here. If, when you meet me, I'm like what you expect me to be, I get positive feedback that you "got" or "experienced" what I wrote about. If there were less of me in the book, or a "prettified" me, it would stand between us in communicating what I am talking about. A *Whole Earth Catalog* without the pages describing the production process and costs is a *Part Earth Catalog*.

Many authors, like Joyce, attempted to keep such a distortion process from affecting their work, but I question their success. In my own case, I have tried to write with all the blemishes and the nasty parts of my personality left in. I tried not to put them in here just for counterbalance or effect, but simply left them in wherever they appeared. Since most of this book was tape recorded, I have corrected the English, because there is a distinct difference between the way the eye hears and the way the ear hears, and a book, appropriately, should be written the way the eye hears. That's what I tried to do. I had hoped when I started that somebody who meets me after having read this book would have a fair understanding of what I am like.

After I completed writing this book and spending many hours with Salli working line by line to make my meanings more explicit, we began the processes of applying the writer's Occam's Razor: "Can this be said in a simpler way?" First Salli and I did it, then Wally Thompson, President of Word Wheel, did it, then Sharon Daniels, whom I've lived with for the past three wonderful years, did it, and finally Charlotte Mayerson of Random House. Each time I had to bow to the overwhelming logic that it did "make more sense" with this or that change in wording. The end product is much more readable. However, in the process of changing only 10 to 15 things per page for the sake of easier reading, part of me has not come through. You should know that in case you meet me; the goal of getting through to the reader with all my blemishes was sacrificed on the altar of reason.

On the other hand, a lot more of me comes through because of the process Word Wheel uses in putting a book together. Salli and I went to a local bookstore one afternoon and looked at an enormous variety of books. We picked the size we wanted, and the type face, and we got an idea about layout possibilities. The first chapter was given to John Martinson of CSC/Pacific in Palo Alto to be keypunched as a deck of IBM cards. It was returned to us as a computer printout for corrections and proofing. The printouts from John's program (called *Magnuscript*) look like ordinary typed pages.We gave it back to him with instructions for the typeface (Palatino), type size (11 point), leading between lines (2 points), and the width of the column (26 picas). John made the corrections on the cards and went through a computer processing routine which ultimately produced the manuscript on punched paper tape with all the proper typographic codes. The tape was taken to a phototypesetting machine, which Salli and I visited, where type is generated on a roll of photographic paper. This is later removed from the machine and developed. (It looks beautiful but smells horrible at that time.)

178

Salli and I used the first results of this process to do a mock-up. A T/square, razor blade, and the simple process of waxing the back of the paper yielded a result that gave me as much pleasure as I've ever had—seeing my own first chapter laid out the way I wanted it. It's a whole new creative area for an author to participate in, with immense rewards and a feeling almost of giving birth.

Later we chose the places to put the photos, Salli's drawings (one by Lisa Hewey), together we created the cover design, and sent the whole thing off to Random House with the complete computer printout. After they had made some editorial suggestions we had the complete set of keypunched cards put in the Stanford University computer, in the system known as SPIRES, run by one of the geniuses of the computer age, Ed Parker (Ph. D.). The material is now available to anyone who wants to pay the phone bill for connecting his or her terminal to the SPIRES system, plus the minimal computer running time. The challenge (to you who are reading this on a terminal) is to devise a good indexing system to get the specific information you want more efficiently than is possible with a table of contents or conventional index.

The finances of the book evolved very slowly and weren't final until the last material was sent to Random House. Part of this was due to the newness of Word Wheel and part to plain old "good process." Salli and I went to New York to talk to publishers, since all of Word Wheel and many people they consulted thought this would be a fairly large selling book of interest to a broad market (ranging from sales forecasts of 75,000 to 500,000 paperbacks). Word Wheel tailors their marketing to the nature of the book; if it's for a small market, they distribute it themselves from the West Coast. If it's a specialized group of readers, they distribute through specialized channels. In this case, with a large potential market, they chose to distribute through a large New York publisher. Salli and I selected two publishers. One was Doubleday, which made a very generous offer to act as distributor by agreeing to buy finished books from Word Wheel in fixed amounts for just under 30% of the retail price (the first order was to be 25,000 paperbacks and 4,000 hardbacks). The other was Random House, which offered to be a co-publisher and divide profits 50-50 with Word Wheel. Under this plan, which was finally selected, Random House prints the book from our camera-ready pages, deducts that cost from the sales revenue, then subtracts the payments (to me, Point, Jug, etc.) and distribution costs, leaving the profit. With Word Wheel's half of the profit, 10% is given to Salli for her role in creating the book, a role we came to call "the midwife," and the rest goes to finance other books.

The final decision on division of the royalties between Jug and myself was potentially difficult. I didn't want to be in the position of telling a friend what I thought his contribution was worth when the consequences of higher praise would be less royalty to me. The solution was to let the board of Word Wheel make the decision since they had a much more objective view.

Word Wheel suggested ten percent of my royalties as Jug's share. Jug preferred to take an advance and seven and a half percent of royalties. I settled on giving 30% of my royalties to POINT. (POINT is a public foundation, so donors are entitiled to a 30% deduction, that is up to 30% of one's income.) This significantly reduces the taxes on the money we actually received and generates funds for others to use.

JAPAN

I visited Japan about a month after I finished writing this book, staying three weeks, nearly all of it in Kyoto. I am unabashedly in love with the Japanese, and had I been there before, this book would have been filled with all kinds of stories about Japan and allusions to the great way Japanese do things. Three things particularly struck me:1) Here is a spectacular industrial economy that is not built on individual competition, 2) The absence of Puritanism in Japan seems to be associated with their greater honesty and openness in dealing with money, and finally 3) We have a great deal to learn from Japan, particularly in terms of money.

First, I have long known as an economist that Japan is the fastest growing and most important force in the dynamics of world economic growth, but until I saw it with my own eyes I couldn't imagine how wealthy she has become. The surprising thing is that this has been achieved by a people whose culture is the antithesis of ours in terms of individual competition. The typical Japanese spends all of his life trying to avoid competitive situations, trying to smooth over potential confrontations, avoiding aggressive behavior, and enjoying his "place" in society. Greed, status-seeking, and ostentation, as we know them, are very hard to find in Japan. So I learned that national economic success need not be tied to personal competition, as is the case in nearly all the Western World.

Second, in talking to many Japanese and to Americans living in Japan, I concluded that most Japanese would recognize the Seven Laws of Money and acknowledge them readily. In fact, they might even view them as "obvious," very much as they viewed our Western discoveries of "non-verbal communication" and "behaviour in public places" as obvious, since they have always been fully aware of these. In terms of giving and receiving the Japanese have very openly calculated the Seven Laws in minute detail. How can this be? My theory is that our Puritanism blinds us to many things, including the nature of money. For centuries we denied the existence of man's sexual-sensual qualities and have been stunned by the recent revelations of its significance. In general, I find that we Westerners also blind ourselves to the whole world of non-verbal, non-rational experience

Well, that's the outline of the theory. I connect Japanese openness about money relationships with their sensualism, as reflected in their food, public baths, incredible gardens and marvelous textiles; and I connect our money blindness with our pervasive but dying Puritanism.

Third, we've got a lot to learn from Japan. I'll only mention two examples.

(1.) There is no tipping in Japan. It made me realize what tips mean. We tell ourselves that tips are rewards for doing a good job, a reward-punishment thing. Then why do we only have tips in job categories where people are expected to be servile—say taxi drivers and waiters, as compared to plumbers or doctors? It's because this is a vestige of slavery experiences and of our contempt for certain ways of earning a living, not reward-punishment.

(2.) The prices of meals and a sample (or picture) of the food is displayed outside of nearly all restaurants in Japan. This really makes sense! No mystery about what your meal will be like or what it will cost.

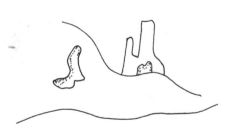

Our Children and Money

Our children learn early that money is dirty, to not put it in their mouths. Many are told that people steal and rob for want of money. They see us, their parents, their guides, rape the land that nourishes us. How we obtain our money and how we disperse it is fascinating to our children.

We encourage our children to save; we encourage them to share. We give them allowances. Some set up trust funds in their names. We work long hours and are too tired to spend time together with our children, and we tell them we do it to earn money to send them to college.

This book originated with a question. A very important question.

How can we parents and teachers cope with supporting our own schools?

Michael has given us some hints, some guidelines that spill out to every facet of our lives. I would like to end all of this with a question.

What are we teaching our children about money?

On Women and Money

It is the men in our society who run the banks, who are our investment counselors, our lawyers, our accountants. It is the men who "take care" of our money for us. Too long have we dealt only with the Thursday supermarket sales, the good buys on kids shoes. We have been imprisoned by our ignorance of money. It is time we break out and do something about this spoiled system under which we live. We have begun our sexual liberation through our own self-pleasuring. Let us continue our political and economic liberation through another form of pleasuring, the kind gained by being informed. The economic climate, to say the least, is highly unfavorable to females, and as long as this is so we will continue to feel oppressed. I look forward to the day when a woman will write a book that will help us deal with our own unique money problems.

I very much want other women to read this book.There are important clues to developing a healthy attitude toward a subject too long enshrouded with mystery. Part of the reason I helped Michael put together the material for this book was to get over my own fears of dealing with money. I used to use up a lot of energy trying to avoid money; fear was ripping me off, fear was keeping me down. I now know that money is like anything else. Money has its own laws, and once you understand them they are no longer in the realm of the unknown, they become tangible, they become possible to deal with. And the rules can be changed. It has been a delight to work on an equal basis with a man, each of us bringing our own unique talents, each pooling what we know so that we might learn together. It has been very rewarding to ask for a fair money return on my work investment.

On Making This Book

This book has a history worth sharing; published by Word Wheel, a group of four very different individuals with a common commitment—to publish books with the full participation of the authors. Writing a book involves so much more than fingers and typewriter. The design of the cover, the size of the pages, the paper, the type that feels right for a particular book are all important. Most publishers don't have the time or staff to give a writer a chance to learn the whole process of creating their book. Michael had something to say, and we wanted to help him say it.

Michael and I formed an alliance. We grew a precious work bond between us. We didn't follow any of the traditional formulas for book making; we made up our own to suit our own needs. This way of working together was so rewarding and such an integral part of the creation of *The Seven Laws of Money* that I would like to share a bit of the process. Michael had a lot to say, but not being experienced in the art of writing he decided to talk it out. He talked into a tape recorder and I gave him my best ears.

When we got the transcripts back Michael's lucid observations were muddled and garbled, although the basic concepts were there. We decided that I would read aloud so that we could both hear where the problems were. We ended up with impossible scribbled pages and the feeling of being at an impasse; neither of us could type twenty words a minute!

Sharon rescued us out of love and played red cross nurse long enough to renew our spirits. We kept her company as she typed into the night.

During this time we trucked down to Palo Alto to interview Richard Raymond about why elephants don't have money, had Stewart Brand over for lunch to interview him about everything. We debated over the merits of various sentences. Ate together, took motorcycle rides together, were discouraged, elated. When we had finished, we pushed the pages from us as after a good meal, and Michael was immediately discouraged. We need an editor! Someone with objectivity! Wally Thompson, President of Word Wheel to the rescue.

We felt relieved and satisfied when the first chapters were sent up from Palo Alto. Our energies rejuvenated. We haunted the bookstores, feeling our way through all the different sizes and shapes books can fit into. We found someone to do the cover whose work we liked. It all fit together. A total process. A good journey.

FINIS!
FINIS
FINIS!

Our Alliance

What is a Briarpatch Society?

In an ultimate sense, the Briarpatch Society consists of people learning to live with joy in the cracks. But, more particularly, if you are positively-oriented and doing (or actively seeking) Right Livelihood, even willing to fail young, and concerned with the sharing of resources and skills with members of an ongoing community (or affinity group), and especially if you see yourself as part of a subsociety that is more committed to "learning how the world works" than to acquiring possessions and status, then you must be a *Briar.*

So howdy, Briar.

If you enjoyed this book and feel close to the Briarpatch I would like to suggest a few things.

There is a *Briarpatch Review* that deals with:
—learning to use money as a tool
—the finding of right livelihood
—joining a community trying to discover a new economics

It's at 330 Ellis Street, San Francisco, California 94102, if you want to subscribe.

Send us your ideas, feelings, experiences and reactions to the Seven Laws. Share and we will try to pass on your sharing to others. (Same Menlo Park address.)

Try some playful experiments with your friends; improvise and create with the Seven Laws and let us know the outcomes.

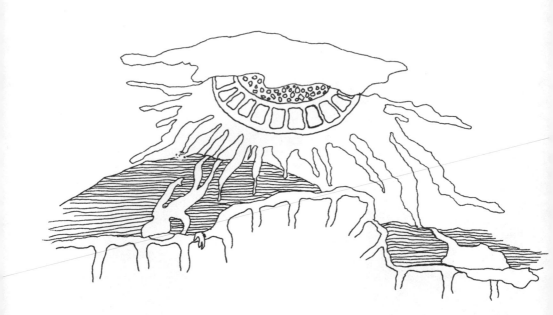

Index